The Human
Behind the Controller

The
Human
Behind the Controller

A Look Into the World of
Competitive Smash Bros. and Esports

Kevin Hu

First Edition: January 2019

Cover Design by Kevin Hu
Cover Photography by Javier Leyvas
www.javileyvas.com

ISBN 978-0-578-42582-5 (paperback)
ISBN 978-0-578-43174-1 (ebook)

Published by Kevin Hu
www.kevinkaywho.com

To all the people I've met in the Smash 4 community.
The Hawaii community, Hold it Down!, San Diego, SoCal,
DK Discord, and to the thousands of people I've crossed
paths with on my travel adventures.

Smash 4 was a blast. Thanks for being a part of it all.

Contents

3, 2, 1, GO!

Hey there! By picking up this book, you're giving esports a chance, specifically the classic yet nontraditional fighting game series *Super Smash Bros.* and more specifically for the iteration *Super Smash Bros. for Wii U.* In this modern day world of rising esports, there are millions of people who just see esports as "glamorized video gaming." A waste of time. Not real sports. A risky career choice, if it can even be considered one. This book is here to show you why you should give esports a chance. With that goal in mind, I'm assuming you are reading this for one of these reasons:

1. You're a gamer yourself! You're interested in what a fellow aspiring esports player has to say. You're bound to find plenty of relatable content that will help you out on your own journey whether you want to make the dive into competitive gaming seriously or if you're already a regular competitor and open to check out the mindset and perspective of a fellow gaming friend.

2. You're a parent or guardian of a child who is nothing but passionate about games. This book will help in getting a perspective of what it means when your child is always going to their friend's house or to the nearest card shop. Even if

you decide to spectate an event, it can be difficult to truly understand why so many people gather together just to prove that they're decent at video games without having a good talk with a competitor—I hope to be that guy to open up the conversation if no one has done so already.

3. This book simply looks interesting. (Thanks!) You might be wondering why video gamers have the audacity to put the letter 'e' in front of an activity that asks of athletic ability when all they're doing is pressing buttons in a chair. Or maybe you want to take a look behind the scenes of a unique way of life. You might be in for a surprise!

Regardless of who you may be, I thank you for having an open mind and checking out one of the most controversial yet rising fields out there. This book is a mixture of both a self-help book and a memoir and with it comes the craziest life lessons I've picked up along the way as a competitor, helping me conquer not only the game of Smash but also the game of life. As your representative of the Smash community, a group of passionate people who play, hang out, and even travel around the world, not for the money but to enjoy a hobby we love, I hope this book opens your eyes towards an often stigmatized passion, maybe even piquing your interest in playing video games for the long term.

If you're not familiar with the game at all without having touched any iteration of the series, the next section should give you a basic enough understanding to grasp the concepts available in this book. Otherwise, feel free to skip to the main chapters. Happy reading!

So... What is Smash?

Super Smash Bros., or simply "Smash," is a 2D fighting game series created by the Nintendo franchise, under the direction of creator

Masahiro Sakurai[1]. However, there are several twists that separate this fighting game from others. Smash is this amalgamation of all of the Nintendo characters you can think of, from Mario to Pikachu, from Donkey Kong to Zelda, from Kirby to Samus, the list goes on. There is a surprisingly large cast of 58 characters in *Super Smash Bros. for Wii U*; in comparison, there are 34 characters in the *Street Fighter V*, 32 fighters in *Dragon Ball FighterZ*, and 43 in *Tekken 7*, all popular fighting games released within the past three years.

Every fighting game has some definition of a character's current health, usually in hit points dropping per hit. However, in Smash, health is represented by a rising percentage value from 0 to 999%, with every player starting at 0%. The higher the number, the farther an attack sends an opponent—this is referred to as "knockback." On average, a character is expected to lose a life, or in this series, lives are referred to as "stocks," when they reach 100%. It isn't surprising, however, if you lose a stock after taking much more, or even much less, than 100%. Sometimes a player loses a stock after taking 200%; other times a player dies even at 20% if the opportunity ever presents itself.

Each match is played on a floating stage in an invisible box, usually just outside the range of one's TV screen. Once your character gets knocked outside of this box—the boundaries making this box is referred to as the "blast lines," and the area beyond these boundaries is called the "blast zone"—you lose a stock in stock mode, the standard mode in competitive play, or you lose a point in timed mode. This means you can't just whittle away at your opponent's health. You need to come up with a strategy to land the final blow or the official term in this game "KO" for knockout. You can do this either by hitting them with a move so strong that they're sent immediately into the blast zone or by knocking

---

1   Masahiro Sakurai is a Japanese video game director and designer who came up with not only this series but also the *Kirby* series.

them off the stage—or simply phrased as "offstage"—and preventing them from coming back. Most fighting games do not have a floating stage where you can fall off and die early, so stages are a significant part of competitive play in this game. Simply returning to the stage after getting hit is one of the biggest differences between Smash and the more traditional fighting games.

Another difference between Smash and other fighting games is the freedom of movement and the variety of stages that have different layouts. In most fighting games, the two players are constantly facing each other in a fairly secluded box. In Smash, you can go anywhere you want around the entire stage regardless of the opponent, even underneath the stage if you want to. Smash's multiple stage layouts provide a variety of strategies, with properties ranging from the number of platforms around the stage to the size of the invisible box. In most other fighting games, aesthetics is usually the main if not the only difference among stages.

With these differences, a new sub-genre of fighting games emerge: platform fighters. The variance between Smash and traditional fighting games is so vast that there's a rather large controversy of whether the former qualifies as an actual fighting game. These traditional fighting games such as *Street Fighter*, *Tekken*, and *Mortal Kombat* are known to be one collective group dubbed as the "fighting game community" or FGC, but it's still quite ambiguous at the moment as to whether Smash is considered to be a part of this community. (In recent times though, Smash has been more accepted as part of the FGC.) To ensure clarity, people often use the term "Smash and the FGC" when referring to all fighting games. More platform fighters have joined the gaming collection alongside Smash lately, including *Rivals of Aether*, *Brawlout*, and *Icons: Combat Arena*, and I suspect that the rise of these games will have people considering all these parties as one collective fighting game community in the near future.

Smash is becoming the next big esport, especially with the newest iteration *Super Smash Bros. Ultimate* out on the Nintendo Switch. Interested? Give the game a shot, or at least hear what its players have to say. You might just be pleasantly surprised.

Chapter One

Just a Competitor

Super Smash Bros. for the Nintendo 64. Kids' dreams were coming alive in 1999. Characters from their favorite franchises would duke it out when no other game had even considered the thought of crossovers. No gaming company would dare create a game where Mario would be fighting Pikachu. Smash was by far the hottest game of the year. Every gaming kid that year had put in at least a hundred hours playing their favorite Nintendo representative. Nobody could have seen what was to come of this series a decade later, let alone two.

Two years later, Smash's second iteration *Super Smash Bros. Melee* came out for the Nintendo GameCube. Since its inception in 2001, it had always been a popular game, but it was nowhere near becoming an esport. Esports wasn't even a term. Back then, players were just players, nothing more. Competitive gaming wasn't considered a profession. Nobody even attempted to make a career out of it. People just played it for the love of the game, even the very best. Organizers hosted tournaments in their basements, and people found out about these tournaments solely through word of mouth (social media wasn't even an existing term).

Players chugged along CRTs and GameCubes to every tournament they attended to provide setups for everyone to use. Nobody minded as long as they got to play the game they love.

Fast forward to 2008 when the third iteration *Super Smash Bros. Brawl* launches on the Nintendo Wii. Unfortunately, most of the Melee competitors deemed it to be too slow of a game to enjoy competitively, so Brawl tournaments did not make big waves as Melee tournaments did, despite being the latest technology. Brawl's numbers would never match up to those of Melee's. Melee players would still continue to carry their CRTs and GameCubes to others' homes; driving their outdated technology across states and checking in their TVs as carry-ons on airplanes just to play a classic. If you ever see a CRT in 2019, the owner probably plays Melee.

Despite Brawl's controversy of how good of a competitive game it was, numbers for both games would continue to rise. Online forums started to rise (before Facebook was a notable form of social media), where people would find out about prestigious national tournaments. The term "esports" was slowly starting to surface, and few people (probably fewer than a dozen) now tried to make a living out of winning tournaments, thanks to these rising numbers. Numbers escalated quickly in other games like League of Legends and Call of Duty, but unfortunately not so much in Smash. The best of the best would barely scrape by, but they didn't mind as long as they got to play. After all, nobody in this day and age ever considered the dream of gaming for a living to be possible.

In 2014, the basis for this book was released: *Super Smash Bros. for the 3DS* and *Super Smash Bros. for Wii U*. While these two games were titled differently, they shared almost all of the same features, but they were simply on different consoles—they may even connect to each other if desired. These games were unofficially accepted by the community known as "Smash 4" as being both the fourth iteration as well as a pun for "Smash for [the 3DS and Wii U]," sometimes stylized as "Sm4sh." Everybody that played Brawl switched over to Smash 4, as the engine in these two games felt similar compared to Melee. Smash 4 was undeniably an upgrade from Brawl: everything was faster, and characters were more balanced. However, the majority of Melee players still stick to their own game. They truly believed Melee was, and still is, the greatest Smash game of all time. Melee's engine required much higher precision, as it was much faster-paced, but those who could master the fundamentals of Melee could never switch off to a slower version. Regardless, you would often see both a flat-screen monitor with a Nintendo Wii U in the same room as a CRT with a Nintendo GameCube.

The term "esports" was starting to spread across the world. Esports teams started forming and picking up Smash players—for both Melee and Smash 4. Tournaments garnered enough entrants to warrant the use of hotel ballrooms, convention centers, and even basketball arenas. The recognition for Smash as an esport rose faster than ever. Advances in technology helped the world of esports rise as a whole, such as the video sharing platform *YouTube* and the live streaming platform *Twitch*. Competitors who wanted to make a living out of Smash now have multiple channels of income outside of tournaments, thanks to creating content for these platforms. People loved getting to know their favorite player on Twitch as they watched the players being themselves, whether they were playing Smash for fun, playing other games, or streaming their everyday lives outside their home.

Despite the gradual rise of esports over the past decade, there was one thing that was slowing down Smash's numbers as compared to other competitive games: Smash never had any developer support. It's crazy to hear that until recent years, Nintendo had the notoriety for not supporting the competitive side of the game they created, even going as far as trying to stop a national event from live streaming and promoting their own game. All other games loved to promote the "esports" side of their game, creating official leagues and circuits, ensuring their game remains balanced through periodic patches and updates, and providing tournaments pot bonuses that communities could never obtain otherwise. For example, the lead developing company of *Street Fighter*, Capcom, has hosted a series of international tournaments, the "Capcom Pro Tour," annually since 2014. The 2018 edition of this tour featured a prize pool of $600,000, numbers Smash can only dream of.[1]

This lack of support left everything in the hands of the fans, including organizing tournaments, marketing, gathering money for prizes, and bringing in the best players. This kept the Smash scene in a grassroots environment where everything was community-driven. The rationale from Nintendo is that they had wanted to keep the Smash series as a family-oriented party game, not a competitive esports platform. While this is an understandable justification, it was unfortunate to see that Nintendo did not share the same outlook as tens of thousands of passionate competitive fans. "It just is always a dismay for our parent company to not see a venture in the same golden light we've been viewing it for over a decade," as top Melee player Juan "Hungrybox" Debiedma states[2]. Smash players were hungry to see their game and community thrive; they couldn't wait to see their game catch up with the rest.

* * *

I had played the original game for the Nintendo 64 back in elementary school the year it came out in 1999, but I had only chosen to compete

---

1   https://dotesports.com/fgc/news/capcom-pro-tour-2018-details-21216

2   https://compete.kotaku.com/nintendo-responds-to-smash-bros-pros-callout-wants-to-1796177733

in tournaments when I heard about the competitive scene back in 2010 with Brawl. Once I entered my first tournament, I had no idea what I was getting into for the next eight years and going: a Smash career that comes with more endeavors and emotions than anything that I've encountered in my lifetime.

Notice the use of the word "career" there. The term has been accepted throughout the Smash community as a reference to a Smash player's competitive journey, possibly but not necessarily making an actual profitable career out of Smash. Despite not actually referring to Smash as an occupation, the parallels between one's Smash journey and one's career in any profession are uncanny. You become interested in a particular subject and want to learn more about it, so you give it a shot. You take a few classes (i.e. enter a few tournaments), read up some books or videos, and you prioritize practicing your skill over many other options that life has to offer. The more you devote time to improving this skill, the more attached you become (or alternatively, maybe you drop your career in an attempt to search for other interests, which is just fine too). In the end, this journey truly becomes your lifestyle, whether it be in business, science, law, art, or really anything you want out of life, including Smash.

I never expected to witness Smash history and watch the amazing stories it had to offer, unfold. I never even thought of traveling across the nation to compete, to be a welcomed member of this community with lifelong friendships, just because of a video game. There have been so many moments in Smash that were insane to witness: including watching the best in the world fight against the best player in Japan, watching the best player from Mexico rise to the #1 player in the world as he struggled to obtain a visa to compete internationally for half of the game's lifespan, celebrating a top ten player's first national tournament win after over three years, and oh, so many more stories to tell. Outside of spectating, every competitor has their own story to tell in their years of entering tournaments regardless of skill level: winning their first tournament match, beating a notable player for the first time, beating a player for the first time whom you've lost to dozens of times before (known as a "demon" or "bracket demon"), getting recognized as a top ten player in your city or region, and so many more feelings of accomplishment, and the failures it took to get there.

Being a part of the Smash community means more than just competing, or perhaps instead of competing to some. There is just so much talent in this community outside of playing video games. Some make amazing artwork and travel across the nation just to sell Smash fan art. Some are videographers who specialize in a specific topic in Smash: maybe sharing tips and tricks as being the best player of a specific character, or just having amazing humor and creating entertaining skits for the masses. Some like to live stream, playing Smash either by themselves while practicing execution or playing in the online matchmaking system, playing with local or online friends, or just playing with viewers who stumble upon their channel. Some thrive off simply supporting their favorite player, often stopping by their stream and donating hundreds to see a skilled player who is rarely able to compete do well. Some like to host events knowing that with their help they enable the majority to do what they love. There is so much talent from a plethora of backgrounds bound by one community, all who serendipitously met each other through a video game.

As competitive gamers, many of us strive for one thing: not necessarily to win the money or the trophy, but to simply be the best at what we do. To put in so much effort into something we are so passionate about and having the results to prove our worth. To take pride in all of the hard work we put in. The beauty of this concept lies in the fact that it doesn't apply only to Smash or even video games, but to anything we aspire to in life. Some want to be the best athlete; others want to be the best musician. What makes Smash any different? As long as we never settle, that's what makes life worthwhile.

This journey will be a rough one. Players are losing games left and right, feeling disappointed and thinking they'll never reach their goals. Everyone will at multiple points in their Smash career feel like a failure. Oftentimes, the goal will feel impossible. There are so many obstacles in the way, hundreds if not thousands of obstacles that one cannot even fathom. There is so much depth to this game that you could never truly understand it all, but if you dare try, you'll discover that one thing that begins your downfall, over and over. You might even be doing well for a few days until suddenly, you start dropping matches nobody expects you to lose, and you start wondering how in the world did that happen for weeks to come.

At the same time, there are those who start fighting those obstacles. Those are the ones who go in with the mindset of wanting to improve, to win, to fight against all nerves and doubts in their head. If they can get good at this game, why can't I? Fight for the recognition, fight for the glory, fight for the family and friends you encounter along the way. Fight to let the world know that you will become the absolute best in whatever you aim for.

With all that said, why listen to me? What separates me from the rest of the community? Honestly, not much. I'm not a professional. I'm not even one of the top five players in my city. That said, I won't be saying much in terms of making esports a career, including how professional players manage their finances and how they find the right team or sponsor. What I do have to offer, however, is a relatable perspective of stories that stem from the first platform fighter series in history. If you do encounter a book here and there about esports, it'd be from a professional. While their perspective is just as worthwhile, my perspective aims to relate to people just like myself—people who go to school, have a day job, etc. but want to make the most of their free time into mastering a hobby. You don't need to become a professional to benefit from the competitive lifestyle, and perhaps that's the most beautiful thing about Smash. I welcome you with open arms not only to hear the stories I have to offer, but maybe even join me in the same tournament one day.

This one video game has surprised me with a journey of self-discovery that I didn't know I needed, of traveling across the country to dozens of regions just to play video games, of meeting hundreds if not thousands of people just like myself who love the game, and simply want to become the best we can be. Hundreds of other Smash players share this similar experience of training to become the best and traveling to compete, but I would love to be the one to share what our community goes through and what we have to offer to the world, from the eyes of a little-better-than-average player that hopefully makes these stories feel more real.

Sounds interesting? I hope you stick around because there's plenty to share. Before I continue, I'd just like to give a quick thanks to Nintendo, and a special thanks to Masahiro Sakurai, the creator of this wonderful fighting game. Without them, this book, and the past few years of my life would not have happened. That said, how in the world could fictional characters like Mario and Pikachu fighting each other change a person's life? Well, let's find out!

Chapter Two

The Cure to Shyness

I grew up in an average, typical Asian home in the paradise we call Hawaii. Everything I did growing up was rather average for an Asian American kid: I took Chinese school on Sundays, I enrolled in the school concert band, I took tutoring lessons at Sylvan Learning Center because I didn't get a 4.0 one quarter in middle school, I was president of my high school math team, and I did chores not for allowance but for the sake of not getting grounded. I grew up with first-generation parents having come from China in their early adulthood, living with a fair family income while they worked in the foodservice industry in Waikiki. While they were rather conservative with their spending, I was even more conservative as a person. My parents were the perfect balance of being strict and lenient, allowing me to live through a pretty great childhood.

During the elementary school years, I played video games only when the family went over to my grandparents' house on my mother's side. To this very day, my grandparents and I can unfortunately barely communicate with one another—being a typical Chinese American who can understand most Chinese words, but without much coming out no matter how much Chinese I studied—so my older brother and I would just play whatever was around while my parents and grandparents talked to each other. We played with whatever toys we collected through Happy Meals and Kids Meals, Legos, Hot Wheels, and any other childhood toys you could think of. If it were a good day, we were allowed to touch the video games: the magical Game Boy handheld, and the even more amazing Super Nintendo console, but only for an hour or so per visit. I would usually tackle the Game Boy first and my brother would take the Super Nintendo, and we often switched later in the hour. After our time was up, back to those inanimate clunks of plastic we called toys. Why my grandparents had all those video games, we had no idea. How they knew what games we'd like, or what games were popular, we had no idea. These are grandparents who came over to Hawaii from China around their 40s we're talking about here, who in this day still barely knows any English. Because they had everything we wanted, however, we never had any of these consoles in our own home for the longest time, and unfortunately for us, we never went over that often—about once or twice a month.

Since our resources were so limited, I grew up with just a few Nintendo games. The earliest ones I remember include *Motocross Maniacs* and *Tetris*, with some lesser-known games here and there. The one series that consumed my childhood, however, was none other than the *Pokémon* series. I would play through all of *Pokémon Red*, *Blue*, and *Yellow*. I had no idea why my grandparents bought me all three but I played them all (maybe one or two for my brother, but he barely played them). On the Super Nintendo, my go-to game was *Super Mario World*. This game was so difficult for me (I was five!) that I think I took an entire year or two just to finish this. The day I finally beat the final boss Bowser, I cheered so hard during a family dinner, only to have everyone ignore my accomplishments and carry on with their food and conversations. *Super Mario RPG* and *Mario Kart* were masterpieces as well, especially for their time.

By the end of elementary school, I finally got myself a Game Boy Color to bring along with me wherever my family went, and I continued my Pokémon fandom with the Gold version. This tradition carried on throughout practically the next decade and a half, playing every generation's worth of games. I got so carried away that I even delved into the competitive Pokémon scene, learning the depths of effort values[1], natures, the need for creativity, and the psychology behind rock-paper-scissors decision-making within every turn, all via online simulators. This lasted until my final college years when the passion had finally died out due to simply greater interests and priorities (and the notorious amount of luck involved, but let's not go into that).

Around the same time I got my Gold version, my brother and I were gifted with the Nintendo 64 in the comfort of our own home, and the first game we got for it was *Pokémon Stadium 2*. We even bought the Game Boy Transfer Pak that would allow us to import our Pokémon from the handheld games to use, realizing that rental Pokémon in the N64 game would never do the trick if we actually wanted to win. I remember the feeling when I accomplished that game 100%. While it took ages, I finally became the greatest Pokémon master in the world, or so my ten-year-old self would say.

---

1   In the *Pokémon* series, "effort values" or "EVs" refer to attributes that raise specific stats of an individual Pokémon. While these attributes are generally ignored in a casual gameplay, these EVs help grow Pokémon in competitive tournaments to focus their stats on their strengths, ensuring that each Pokémon is fighting at their utmost potential. For example, if a Pokémon were designed to defend, EVs would typically go towards health and defense rather than attack points.

Not too long after, my brother and I were gifted with the most coveted game during its time: *Super Smash Bros.*

All the kids were talking about it! We didn't realize it at that time, but we all loved the creativity behind all these Nintendo characters finally duking it out like we all had in our imaginations. We finally got to witness Mario fighting Kirby, Pikachu fighting Link, even two Donkey Kongs fighting each other. Given my Pokémon and Mario background, I already knew at that moment that this was the game for me, and I'm sure others shared this exact same thought.

This was the first game that my brother and I played together consistently. We hadn't played any of the Pokémon games together— maybe once or twice using rentals in Stadium, and we probably only raced a few times in Mario Kart (one of us giving up every time thanks to childhood tantrums). We tried out the 2-player mode in Super Mario World only to realize that this meant alternating between stages, not two people playing at once. Smash was the perfect opportunity for us to play games together, and those matches were just so great.

Even when my brother didn't want to play Smash, I was still able to play through a bunch of the single-player modes, and at that time fighting the computer opponents was the toughest challenge. My friends would always brag whenever they completed single-player mode with a specific character, and I remember being envious because I wanted to be the best with every single character. I actually don't even remember sticking to one character at that time. All I can recall was trying out my pal Pikachu from Pokémon Yellow (having trained him up to past level 80!) and failing miserably due to not being able to use his Quick Attack, his main recovery option if I wanted to make it back to the stage after getting hit.

When the GameCube and Super Smash Bros. Melee came out,

everything was more exciting than ever before. It was so great that I don't even think we bought any other games for the GameCube; we just rented everything else from Blockbuster. While my brother and I played a bunch of matches at home, I also got to play several games in school when the "cool teacher" in middle school brought the game in to his own classroom during lunch. I remember getting so excited every time Melee was brought up in conversation, and I tried to bring up that topic as often as I could. I even remember having to write a short two paragraphs in 5th grade writing about a favorite activity and giving it a rating. I gave Melee a 9 out of 10. When the teacher passed the assignments around for classmates to read and grade, they would all ask me, "Why not 10/10?" I responded confidently, "Because there'll be an even better Smash game in the future."

So much of my time had been invested in this game during my prepubescent years. Going through all of the single-player event matches (mini-games in Smash), trying out all the characters, playing against my brother whenever he was interested—there was unlimited replay value in this game and there was just so much to do. Fighting the same characters over and over never got old, and neither did losing to Giga Bowser, an "evolved" form of Bowser, about five times greater in size. I remember taking a full month to finally bring him and his minions Mewtwo and Ganondorf down—by running away and shooting projectiles with Samus from the *Metroid* franchise. Despite the name of this game, I could never win that event if I ever tried fighting close-range. I just couldn't. I even gave my trusted pal Pikachu a second shot; I still couldn't use Quick Attack to save my life. I even tried to use all the other Pokémon available—Jigglypuff, Pichu, and Mewtwo—expecting them to be my saviors since I had such a strong connection with the Pokémon franchise.

While none of them did justice against Giga Bowser, I started getting a feel for Mewtwo more than anyone else in the cast. I started using him for everything: rerunning through all the event matches, playing through all the single-player modes over and over, achieving all the hidden accomplishments, and even beating my friends at school with Mewtwo. I eventually was able to beat Giga Bowser and his gang with Mewtwo, fighting up close as a fighting game should be. Because I was good with a character as cool as Mewtwo, the rarest Pokémon in the franchise, I thought that I was the coolest kid among all my friends who also played Smash, that I was the king of the world.

* * *

I moved to a different high school from everyone else, barring only about four others whom I had never really talked to. All of a sudden, I became the shyest kid in the entire school; no, the entire world. Ask any of my high school friends, or even any classmates, acquaintances even—they'll all agree. I was so shy and became such a socially awkward little boy that I would answer most questions with yes or no just to get out of the situation: "What'd you do last night?" "Yeah." "How was band practice?" "Eh." "How was the homework?" "Yeahhhh." On top of that, almost everyone in high school came from one of two feeder schools excluding mine, so most friendships and cliques were already solidified. It was definitely a struggle trying to fit in, and I was definitely not the coolest kid on the block anymore.

Over the course of my first quarter or two in high school, I was learning that my main way of making friends was through my skills and talents in school. Almost everything I did highlighted this epiphany, and I was trying to take advantage of it just to get noticed. It made sense even back then: people are attracted to others with notable skills because they can use it for themselves, either directly or through purely being entertained, surprised, or envious. People are attracted to success, simply put. The alternative? Trying to make conversation. For me, that was infinitely more difficult, so I had no other choice.

In band, I already stuck out of the crowd for being the only French horn player out of about 60 musicians. People still hadn't approached me, however, they all stuck in their own cliques, and honestly, if I were them, I would have done the same. Why would I try to make new friends when I already have a great group around me? They had only started talking to me once I performed challenging pieces when we were asked to play one-by-one during rehearsal and I would get it down almost perfectly, both technically and musically. According to my band teacher, my only problem was playing as quietly as I was shy, but at least he noticed my attempts at dynamics.

Even my band director noticed my talent and was bold enough to give me, a quiet little freshman, a solo piece to perform in my first high school band concert. This one was in the medley of the Broadway musical *Wicked*, soloing the introduction of "Defying Gravity." It's a quiet intro with almost nonexistent background music, and so I was as exposed as ever. He had the option of giving the solo to the lead senior alto saxophone player (as the horn cues were written in the saxes' sheet music), but he remained confident in my abilities. By the end of the concert, my popularity shined brighter than ever, and I finally had friends I could talk to regularly both inside and outside of the band room since many of my band friends also shared the same classes as me. To this day that song still resonates with me as its message was fully ingrained in me: if you can defy gravity, if you can overcome all odds, nothing can stop you.

This "trick" of showcasing my talents to friends started to pop up everywhere. I'd ace tests and the teachers would brag to the class about it. Students would sometimes grade each others' homework during class and they'd ask me how I figured out a problem. It was omnipresent: my artwork in drawing class, my piano skills that I decided to pick up one day after band practice to play Defying Gravity and video game music (inspired by the "Super Mario Medley" covered by the Video Game Pianist[2]), my presidency in our comfy little math team of never more than a dozen, and similar leadership roles in the National Honor Society. Even my Photoshop and HTML/CSS skills on my MySpace page brought me as much attention as the Jetsam I trained on Neopets did. I was nowhere near a prodigy and I'm definitely not trying to proclaim that I was, but it was rather easy to stick out of the crowd, especially when half of the students in even an honor's class couldn't turn in their homework in time.

Naturally, I sought for similar recognition when I discovered the Melee scene near the end of my freshman year. After school, a guy would bring his GameCube into a classroom—with a teacher who would allow it—and their friends would just play for two hours or so daily. I would give it a shot for several days, one because it was Smash, and two to try to make a friend who wasn't a complete academic nerd like myself.

A few days later I would give up entirely. They were just too good. I don't think I took a single stock (Smash's term for "life") against them, ever. They knew all these advanced techniques that I had never heard of at the time but were commonplace if not required in the competitive Melee scene. Terms like "wavedashing," "L-canceling," "dash-dancing," and "tech-chasing" were foreign. It was way too much information to take in, and from then I had given up completely on Melee, knowing that if I wanted to get as good as them, I would probably have to commit as much time into the game as I did in my studies. As an academic nerd,

---

2   Pianist Martin Leung, whose video "Super Mario Medley" included a blindfolded version of the main theme song and was one of first viral videos back in YouTube's inception in 2004. As of 2018, he still uploads YouTube videos. http://videogamepianist.com/

I knew this wasn't an option, and so there went any chances of being recognized for Melee. To this day, I still can't perform a wavedash, one of the most used advanced techniques in this specific game (but not in any other Smash game).

Fast forward two years and the world was gifted with the most popular game for the Nintendo Wii, *Super Smash Bros. Brawl.* Overall, Brawl is a slower-paced game with much less required technical skill, removing all those aforementioned techniques, but there was still a competitive edge to this game. Now that my friends and I were nearing adulthood, we had quite a bit more freedom, despite having more homework and part-time jobs. Most importantly, we could drive and visit our friends' houses just to play video games. While I didn't have the courage to spend my money on a Wii (once I had a part-time job, my parents never bought me anything gaming related anymore), I was fortunate enough to play Brawl almost every weekend, especially during the summer before my senior year.

My friends and I discovered our interest in Brawl one day when the game was brought into the computer lab after school. Several kids happened to be playing, and we asked if we could give it a shot. I remember being of rather equal skill to my friends, but easily beating the kids whom we requested to play with. From there, almost everything we talked about was of Smash. If it wasn't about school, it was Smash.

Keoni, my number one sparring partner for Brawl, went under the gamer tag "FTL," short for "for the lose" instead of the typical gaming phrase "for the win," or "FTW." Before Brawl, he was still one of my close friends, having been in band and my honors classes, but Brawl was undeniably the turning point in our friendship. We were even fairly equal in Smash skill, growing together as players throughout the years. Most of the time when I was out socializing; if it wasn't hanging out after band practice, I would be visiting his house with a few other friends just to play Smash.

We started pouring hours into this game. Oftentimes I would get to his house at around 11 A.M. and leave ten hours later without a single snack. As unhealthy as it was, during that entire time we were only hungry for more games. After playing every character for a few hours each, I discovered my love for the character Donkey Kong, especially with the fact that Mewtwo did not make a return in Brawl. Donkey Kong wasn't considered the best character, ranked 21st out of 38 characters on the Brawl tier list (a community-made ranking of all the characters in a competitive setting), and I barely even played any of his games, but despite all of that, he just felt so natural in my hands. He could run around surprisingly quickly for his size, and his long arms meant that he could attack people from farther away than smaller characters. He could jump high despite his weight, and he could literally carry his opponents on his back as he walks off the stage. Donkey Kong and I even shared parts of our personality, acting rather carefree yet considered trustworthy by many. I knew even then that if I were to become great at Smash, it would be with Donkey Kong. FTL, on the other hand, had put faith into Princess Zelda, from the *Legend of Zelda* series. Although she was considered the second worst character in the game, FTL put in great work with her and still managed to keep our games even.

In the gaming world, we call the character we specialize in our "main," e.g. "Donkey Kong is my main." The term "main" can also be substituted as a verb for "specialize in," e.g. "I main Donkey Kong." Lastly, this term could also be used in conjunction with the character to describe someone: "That guy is a Donkey Kong main." Alas, Donkey Kong was now indeed my main, and Zelda would be FTL's main. If one invests equal time into two characters, we call those their "co-main," similarly either as a noun or verb. If one invests less time into one or more characters than their main, we call that their "secondary" (also usable as a verb, but not so much as a descriptor for a person, e.g. *not* "he is a Zelda secondary").

The funny thing is that, despite sticking with this carefree gorilla throughout my entire Smash career, I hadn't played through any of the *Donkey Kong Country* games until early 2018. Regardless, I still felt a shared connection with him over the years. As crazy as connecting to a video game character sounds, it's just as common in any other hobby: a digital artist and her tablet and pen, a basketball player and his basketball, a tennis player and her racket. When you're stuck with your tool of choice for hundreds if not thousands of hours, it only becomes natural, but my tool of choice just happens to have a personality as well.

I felt like Donkey Kong and I shared such a connection at an almost spiritual level that I just had to base my gamer alias around him. After playing him for months, I finally settled with the tag "iDK." It's been over half a decade later and it still feels like the perfect tag for me. On top of having "DK" in my tag, it embellishes Donkey Kong's signature move, his "down taunt". He breaks the fourth wall as he faces the screen and shrugs rather expressively. Although this move does not do any damage, it has become such an integral part of my play since 1) it throws off my opponent in such an intense match, and 2) it reminds me that despite wanting to win and become the best so badly, I should have fun and enjoy the ride. With this expression and the fact that my tag was a pun—and I'm a sucker for bad puns—it was perfect for me. (As a bonus, it pairs well with my last name.) Little did I know how much the Smash community would hear of this tag.

Eventually, FTL[3] and I became so good compared to the rest of our

---

3   It is expected to call Smash players by their gamer tags, just like an online persona.

friends that they all lost interest and stopped showing up, similar to my relationship with Melee. As unfortunate as that was, he and I still played for ten or more hours a day, while I still talked to the others at school. This passion started to become a real thing, even more than my entire childhood with Pokémon because I was playing Smash with real friends regularly. I had then wanted to make this a small goal, nothing too serious: to become a great recognized player in the community in Hawaii. I even had a friend with similar goals who wanted to help and grow along the way.

Months of playing in the computer lab and at FTL's home passed, and eventually, we graduated. Most of us were parting ways, but not FTL and me. Little did we know that graduation was just the beginning. What happened to me and Melee was starting to happen all over again.

Chapter Three

University of Brawl

Throughout the summer between high school and college, FTL and I had been putting in the hours. At least every other weekend, we would visit his place to become the best on the island. We recorded videos of our matches while we played with a camera, trying to play as quietly as we could so that the mic wouldn't catch random bursts of laughter (we were too lazy to set up capture cards). With these recordings, we could analyze what we could have improved on. And just like filming yourself when you speak, watching your own play felt embarrassing, but we knew it had to be done. We knew like school, as long as we put in the work, we would get to where we want to be. We knew we could beat anyone that played the game casually, which in hindsight isn't saying much, but not having known about the tournament scene back then, that meant the world to us.

Probably the one thing I was excited for in college was not the freedom, not the choice to study what I wanted, but playing against other college kids in Smash. I imagined plenty of older kids, actual *adults*, being amazing at this game—even more so than the high school kids that would destroy me. I couldn't wait for that challenge. I was even fortunate enough to reside in the dormitories, thanks to a scholarship despite living a mere ten-minute drive away, staying on the island, and attending the University of Hawaii at Mānoa, so all I could think of was playing Smash every weekend, and maybe even some weeknights, against my future roommate and other gamers on our floor.

This is a little humiliating, but I remember two weeks before the first day of school, we were notified of who our roommate was going to be so we could contact them on what we would bring and share in the room. The dormitory staff would pair recipients of the same scholarship together, so from that one fact I knew I could trust him without having met him before, likely being as academic-focused and like-minded, or at least as studious as myself (it turned out that all of the recipients of this scholarship got along well, without a single bad egg). Turns out my new roommate, Jeff, was a valedictorian of one of the top renowned private schools in the state who is at the time of writing studying in medical school. After a chain of logical fallacies (he was a nerd like me, so he must play games like me, which means...), I concluded that I could shamelessly ask him if he plays Smash! *If* he did, he *must* have been as talented as he was erudite—it definitely takes brains to be good at a game with this much depth. It all made sense, at least in my head, and it didn't help that FTL encouraged me to ask him. Jeff admitted that he did play Smash after all. Not a bad way to start a roommate relationship let alone a friendship in general. As a bonus, he was also a fellow Chinese American, so I had a great feeling we would get along easily.

Jeff was already planning on bringing in all the necessities, including a mini fridge and a microwave. In turn, I told him that I could bring all the fun and games including the TV and the Wii, which FTL was ever-so-kind enough to leave at my dorm since he was planning on visiting often after admitting nobody else would come to his house to play Smash anyway, and I didn't own one. Moreover, FTL was equally excited to play against this new group of gamers.

On the first day of school, Jeff and I had already plugged in the Wii and started playing. He wasn't bad, but it was clear that FTL and I had spent way more time on this game than he had. I was admittedly not going to improve much from playing against Jeff, but our session was still enjoyable and we were clearly going to play more throughout the year. Perhaps we'd even hang out outside of the game and dormitory as well.

I was also fortunate to have such a roommate who was as proactive as he was amicable. On the second Monday evening after going back home for the weekend (also living ten minutes away), he brought in a full pan of lemon bars to share with our honors floors, a total of about twenty freshmen in our apartment, and he had asked me to come along to share. Lots of the floormates were appreciative of this welcoming gift, and we started some great introductory conversations from there. Some even planned on visiting our room to hang out later. Even on day one, Jeff would always leave our door open for anyone to stop by, so after that evening lots of people started taking up on our open door invite.

My fortune continued as several floormates also enjoyed playing Smash, both guys and girls. While they were all near Jeff's level, the first day of playing Smash together was foreshadowing a good year and great friendships to come. In the end, it didn't matter how good they were; it was about how much fun I had making friends through this one video game.

Throughout the year, we would alternate between multiple games: Smash, Mario Kart, Mario Party, and Rock Band on a friend's XBox. Gradually we played Smash less and played the other games more. Although none of us wanted to admit it, the fact was that the level gap was becoming too wide for anyone to enjoy the game. Even if I would go solo in a 3 versus 1 fight while choosing the random character select option, I would still win more often than not. As unfortunate as that was, we all enjoyed the other games, as we all hated the blue shell in Mario Kart together and that one lucky person in Mario Party. Rock Band was just amazing in its own right with our unique talents. While I didn't regret any of my gaming time with these friends, my love for Smash was slowly dying as I couldn't find others who both loved the game and also compared in skill.

Almost unsurprisingly, a saving grace had come in at just the right time. Early on in the second semester, FTL had informed me of the annual Smash tournament at the biggest anime convention in Hawaii: Kawaii Kon. He had never attended the convention let alone a tournament before, but he insisted on me joining him in this tournament. The convention hosted both a singles and doubles tournament, with the doubles tournament first on Saturday followed by singles on Sunday, so we figured teaming together would be a great way to debut ourselves before we claimed our throne. (They also held a casual free-for-all tournament with items on Friday, but our school schedules prevented us from attending.) Turns out that this tournament had been running since Brawl's inception two years ago, so we had missed out on quite a bit, but it was never too late. Of course, I would be there.

We walked in on the doubles tournament on a perfect Saturday, not too long after we enjoyed our spring break week. Simply arriving at the scene with plenty of Smashers who are in it to win it felt rejuvenating. There were about 30 individuals hovering along a wall with a few setups. It was an odd feeling of both belonging and isolation, walking into a scene of strangers who shared my biggest hobby. Who knew how the day was going to turn out?

The tournament organizer, or TO, emphatically called everyone in to stop playing their friendlies, or non-tournament matches (known as *casuals* in other fighting game communities), as he was about to go over the rules. I didn't realize this process would be so complex. The tournament (and pretty much all other Smash tournaments) was in a double-elimination format, meaning if you lose to an opponent, you're still in the tournament with one more chance in the loser's bracket. Each match against an opposing opponent would be best of three games, three stocks on an eight-minute timer. Friendly fire would be turned on, meaning teammates could potentially hit each other. The rules provided a restrictive stage list paired with a particular order on how to pick the first stage involving rock-paper-scissors. There was quite a bit to take in, but plenty of veterans were there to help us along the way. Nonetheless, the sheer complexity had already scared us away from winning. After all, how can you win if you don't even know the rules?

Our first match actually ended up being recorded by the TO. Insult to injury? Most likely, until it turns out we were up against two young boys, both in the players and the characters. Two middle school boys teamed up together as Toon Link from the *Zelda* series and Lucas from the *Earthbound* series. FTL and I used our trusted characters: Zelda and Donkey Kong. After the first minute, FTL and I both started to calm our nerves as we realized this would be a free win. While we were a rather solid team as players, it turned out that our characters also paired well. Zelda would throw out projectiles and combos with her magic while Donkey Kong would secure early kills with his raw strength. The TO, "DarkMusician," recognized our talents and talked to us for a bit after that match, encouraging us to check out future tournaments outside of Kawaii Kon. FTL and I definitely gave the suggestion some consideration, but for now, we had to focus on the rest of the tournament.

Later in the day, we played against two guys who were similar to us both in age and skill. "Tita," a Jigglypuff player, teamed with a Lucario player by the tag "Anteh," and each game ended up as a one-versus-one last-stock last-hit situation[1]. Even in a two-versus-one situation, in either team, the solo player would make the comeback and win. Just because a team was losing never meant that they were out; it's never over until it's over. At the end of the set, FTL and I secured the win, and Tita and Anteh did not regret losing such a great match.

After that match, spectators started talking about us. People started calling us Tarzan and Jane thanks to the nature of our characters. Although I don't remember how the rest of the tournament went, I do remember holding our own against the tournament veterans, though we never beat any of them. Thanks to our ability to keep up, however, we were welcomed to the community rather seamlessly.

The next day, however, said otherwise. I had the worst luck in having to fight the guy who was considered the best player on the island during that time. He was part of a crew of young high schoolers who I believed at that time spent all of their free time on this game, possibly every single weeknight, as many others would describe them that way. He went by the tag "WAR," which intrigued me because I found out that day that his tag actually represented his initials. He also entered the tournament representing his crew "GSM," or "Game, Set, Match" (or alternatively "Gimp Style Madness"). GSM was actually known throughout the nation in Brawl for their well-crafted YouTube videos, featuring insane combos that even top players ravished over, and their first combo video "What Rank You"[2] featured a creative setup from WAR's Snake from *Metal*

---

1   A last-stock last-hit, or simply "last-hit," situation is a common term for when both players are one strong hit away from losing the game.

2   "What Rank You" was in reference to Hawaiian Pidgin, as the video showcased Smash players from Hawaii. https://www.youtube.com/watch?v=D4TaJd8uwWg

Gear Solid after breaking an opponent's shield. A few top players today have even admitted to have gotten into Smash after watching WAR and these videos.

Against me, he used a fast and nimble Captain Falcon from the *F-Zero* series. His movement was intimidating, as it was difficult to pinpoint when he would commit to an attack. Pairing that with the fact that I was playing the top player of the state already put me in a disadvantageous mindset, fighting just to stay alive instead of playing to win. While he was quite a personable and charismatic player, I was starting to get flashbacks of Melee in high school, and the whole match felt discouraging. I do remember he kept telling me not to sweat it, especially as it was my first singles tournament match ever.

I sadly don't remember the rest of this tournament either, except having beaten others who played the game much less than my college friends, then losing to another veteran quickly. While the results were discouraging, the tournament acted more as a motivator telling me just how much more work I had to put in if I wanted to keep up with my goal. I now knew where I stood within the competition of Smash Bros. Hawaii.

After that weekend, the veterans started referring me to the website *Smash Bros. Hawaii* where we could find all the information related to our favorite game in our favorite state[3]. Within the website held a forum where I could talk with all the people I just met. All of GSM posted regularly there, as did DarkMusician and his friends. This forum was huge given that Facebook was not well-known at the time, and the primary site for social media, MySpace, didn't provide group forums. On the forum, everyone had their gamer tag as their username, if not in their signature, so I couldn't quite recognize anyone except for the people I

---

3   The website no longer exists since Facebook now covers all of our needs.

met in person. While introducing myself online, I skimmed throughout the forum content for a while, seeing just how much depth was in the game and how much time these people invested into this passion. They also talked about their hobbies outside of Smash and gaming, which was fun to chat in once in a while. Turns out I found the secret goldmine to become not only the best but also to make friends with other gamers.

In addition to all the tips and tricks, the forum contained all the information for future events. They had been hosting monthly tournaments at various venues; you had to know about this website or its members to find out about them. Unfortunately without Facebook, spreading the word was exceptionally difficult, so the Smash community especially DarkMusician was grateful for having found FTL and me that weekend. They had to take advantage of Kawaii Kon's reputation every year to grow the scene, as the convention would draw in an average of five thousand attendees per year at that time[4]. Even in the forum, they would discuss how to advertise, including hanging up flyers around schools and venues with similar audiences. The growth compared to today was especially disappointing, but all of the regulars at that time appreciated the comfort of the intimate community of one to two dozen people.

FTL and I decided to check out the next monthly, at that time held at a venue named Hawaiian Brian's, known for their pool tables, darts, arcade games, and a bar with live music. It was a nice venue with plenty of space, food for purchase, and side activities outside of Smash; most venues cannot even provide any of the three. Smash tournaments were held at this venue for almost a year before they were forced to switch due to lack of participants and fees.

Compared to the Kawaii Kon tournament, this event only consisted

---

4   While Kawaii Kon 2010 brought in about 5000 attendees, Kawaii Kon 2017 held over 12,000 attendees, showing that anime was not planning on slowing down anytime soon: https://en.wikipedia.org/wiki/Kawaii_Kon

of about twenty entrants, so they were able to host both a doubles and a singles tournament on the same day. I felt much more comfortable walking into the venue this time, recognizing almost every face and not being so astonished by the overall skill level. In fact, in the doubles tournament, our first match was once again versus Tita and Anteh. They clearly wanted their revenge, and they were going to fight their hardest against FTL and me for that win.

By the end of the match, we all knew there was an unspoken rivalry among the four of us. We barely won the match a second time, and they were upset for failing to avenge themselves. The funny thing is that in almost every doubles tournament from here on out, we had to play against them and we won every time, despite how close the matches always were. This day made me fall in love with the community, as I finally found people around my level and people I could talk to on a regular basis every time I went to a tournament. Later that day, we found out that Tita and Anteh were actually roommates and invited us to play at their house often. Not only did we all become better players by finally training with others at our level but we also started hanging out outside of Smash, talking about a variety of subjects from career aspirations to performing music.

As an introvert, I had never felt such a feeling. All I wanted to do was play Smash, but for a reason outside of the game: to meet as many like-minded people as possible. I loved how comfortable I felt upon immediately approaching them with a simple hello. I loved how I knew what interests we shared without having to share a single word. Yet despite that, I loved how much I still didn't know about them and how much I would get to know them once we got along. In college, whenever I met someone who shared my major, or even in our school's wind ensemble whenever I talked to people who played the same instrument, I still felt uncomfortable in trying to make friends and finding that starting point of shared interest. I couldn't just talk about how much I liked math and science, or how much I liked a particular composer or song. They simply weren't conversation starters. In addition, it was difficult to find time in the middle of class to start a conversation, except with maybe just one or two people. With Smash, however, there is so much depth within this game that I could talk about it for hours. For someone who couldn't speak more than two words per sentence, everything suddenly became so easy. I still needed some time to feel comfortable enough to start talking about subjects outside of Smash, but there was just so much content in the game that I could go my own pace without feeling rushed.

A month or two later, I started planning my own tournament in the dormitories. I knew there had to be more hidden talent out there. I could meet more people, and I could potentially grow the scene just a little bigger by showing my tournament participants DarkMusician's monthlies. A short talk with my resident advisor (RA) later, we scheduled a tournament two weekends before finals.

Hosting this tournament was just as exciting as playing in it. I had put my limited graphic design skills to use, creating a poster with magnified images of exciting Smash moments such as when someone lands a spike[5]. We even included the Smash Bros Hawaii website, hoping to bring in some potential regulars. The RA helped me in printing out the flyers with the dormitories' printers and hanging them up throughout the apartments, including the ones I did not have access to. In addition, because this was considered a school event, we could not have people paying to enter the tournament to contribute to a prize pot since the school may potentially consider that as gambling. Instead, the RA was

---

5   A spike is an attack that quickly sends the opponent downwards. This is fairly hard to connect, but if the opponent is not directly above the stage, this almost always means a kill.

able to use the school's money to purchase food and gift cards as prizes. While I was thankful for the RA putting in most of the work, I still passed out quarter-page flyers and spread the word to interested colleagues. I also asked people to bring in both monitors and consoles, and Tita and Anteh were willing to provide theirs despite not having the time to participate.

The tournament brought in about twenty people, just as big as the monthly series. I only knew three of them as well, including FTL and two floormates, so the fact that this event had spread out to people outside of my circle was a great sign. Both the RA and I were ecstatic. He got to report to his supervisor a successful event when most RAs hosted events with no more than ten people, while I also got everything I wanted Smash-related. The RA was also able to help call out matches during the event as I taught him how to use the bracket-organizing software called *Tio* (pronouncing it just like "TO" for tournament organizer). Some of my friends helped out as well, making everything run much more smoothly. Everyone was willing to help each other out just so we could all have a great time. While they handled the bracket, I would walk around the room making sure the players knew how the rules worked, as I remembered just how complex hearing the rules for my first time was. I also had enough time to participate in the tournament myself, thanks to everyone's help. Everything was run perfectly even though nobody had handled anything like this before.

Despite none of the competitors ever having heard of the tournament scene, there was a lot more talent than I expected. I couldn't tell if I was more excited about seeing all these players here or if they were more excited about playing in their first tournament. A few hours later, I ended up winning the whole thing, even winning over FTL. It felt like I had cheated the system, having set up the event only to win my own rewards (that the RA provided too!), but in the end, everyone including the RA congratulated me for the well-deserved win. Although nobody besides FTL was a regular competitor, it still wasn't an easy win. Taking first had never felt more amazing.

* * *

That tournament was such a good time that I even hosted a second tournament the following semester in a new dormitory. This event was even bigger and better than last time with similar prizes, with about thirty entrants and six setups. However, while I was improving in this game, so was everyone else. I ended up placing fifth in this tournament, losing to people who had started attending the monthly tournaments between the two dormitory tournaments. Seeing how far we have all come was beautiful; all I could remember was thinking *I did this. I brought all of us together.* After this second tournament, even more, people started showing up to the monthlies, or at least the next Kawaii Kon tournament. I even started hosting my own "Smashfests" regularly—hangout days when people would just come over and play Smash without the stress of a tournament. We would hang out on Friday nights in the dormitory lounge until 2 or 3 A.M., playing until we were absolutely exhausted to the point where we'd fall asleep the minute we touched our beds.

Kawaii Kon kept getting bigger every year, and so did each tournament. We started averaging 40 to 50 people each year for the next four years. The Smash community even brought over a special guest from Southern California, "DEHF[6]," known as the best Falco (from the *Star Fox* series) player in the world. Everyone was trying to bring down DEHF, but nobody could do it. Not even WAR. Around this time, a different player was recognized as the best on the island, also in the GSM crew going by the tag Lethal Trilogy, or LT. Not even he could take down

---

6   DEHF is short for "Does Everyone Hate Falco?"

DEHF—not even close. Knowing that I never stood a chance against the best GSM members, seeing those guys struggle against DEHF opened my eyes to just how much further we *all* have to go[7].

DEHF had started attending Kawaii Kon every year since 2011, as he was the one professional player DarkMusician was close friends with. He and his crew would raise funds each year to have DEHF play with us so that he could share his talents with all of us. Seven years later including in both Brawl and Smash 4, aside from 2017 where he wasn't able to make it, nobody has yet to claim his throne.

FTL and I were only able to team in doubles for one more year, but people were excited to see us back in action in 2011. Fate led us to fight Tita and Anteh yet again, and as always, we had close yet fantastic matches with us securing the win. I had started placing top 16 in singles, which was much better than when I started off by just winning one match. I loved watching my improvement over time. Even if it were over multiple years, it was a constant reminder that no matter what we did, we'll eventually get there. Eventually, I would be able to beat DEHF. Eventually.

Later, at the end of 2011, I wanted to plan something exciting for my 20th birthday. Usually, I just celebrate it by going out for dinner with the family, but Smash made me want something more this time around. I hosted a casual tournament at my home, where my competitive friends could fight their hardest and my casual friends could see how a Smash tournament was run.

Since majority of my friends were at my house just to play Smash casually, I decided to host a doubles tournament with no prize, using a random generator to pair people together. Every competitive player

---

7   The national Brawl scene didn't have a ranking list until 2014 when Smash 4 was released, but in that list, DEHF was ranked number 17 in the world.

happened to pair up with a casual player (if two competitive players ended up together, we planned on rerolling anyway), making everything fair and fun. Tita ended up winning the tournament with one of my dormitory friends who went by the tag Candi. She was just as excited for winning her first tournament as I was the previous year, sharing her excitement with Tita in such a great evening while everyone cheered for them. Since there were only about seven teams, the tournament ran for less than two hours, so we spent the rest of the evening just playing friendlies and having fun.

2012 came along and here I was back again at Kawaii Kon. At this tournament, I remember landing the craziest combo of all time; Hawaii Smash veterans today still remember that very moment. I was against a player who had participated in the tournament scene several times this past year, going by the tag So Desu. He and I shared a special rivalry: we both used Donkey Kong. We had never faced each other in a tournament before, so this match was finally going to settle who the best Donkey Kong on the island was.

In the first match, I secured a convincing win, only losing one stock out of three. However, in the second game So Desu starting controlling the pace and ran off with a significant lead. I ended up being one strong hit away from losing this game, while he was one hit away from losing only his second stock. I manage to sneak in a kill to take his second stock, but I was still in a severe disadvantage. How was I supposed to rack up over an entire stock's worth of damage without taking a hit? Thanks to the positioning of the dynamic stage Rainbow Cruise (where platforms are constantly moving around, albeit at a fixed speed and direction), I somehow managed to pull out a full combo, one hit after another. So Desu had one opportunity to get out of my barrage of attacks, but he threw out an unsuccessful dodging in the air as he kept himself in a dangerous position. My combo ended with Donkey Kong's signature move, "Giant Punch," sending him off the screen at a percentage earlier than usual. Despite him having only received one hit on his last stock before the combo, I stole the game from him[8]. The feeling after was astounding! We had a large crowd behind us witnessing what just happened, perhaps 20 or more teens and young adults, and everyone just shouted "OHHH!" while looking at each other in surprise. "I thought I had that game too, but I'm not even upset! That was just too good," I remember So Desu saying as he smiled. The best part was that this match was being recorded for YouTube, so we could all reminisce about this moment even today[9]. When I left the station, everyone started patting me on the back and just talking to me about their disbelief, lasting an entire ten minutes of congratulations. I didn't care how I did throughout the rest of the tournament; I definitely got more than I wanted out of that day.

Despite the excitement of this tournament, after Kawaii Kon 2012, things started looking grim. Not as many people showed up to the monthlies now. People just weren't as interested in the game, and other life priorities took over. Only a few people from the GSM crew, the best players at that time, would show up. Despite my improvement, I would still consistently place in the last place, so why would others want to join in? Numbers were so small now that we had to move the tournament venue to a tiny computer store, which could comfortably fit only about eight people at once. This computer store was known for being a non-profit gaming organization called *Hawaii Video Gaming League*, or *HVGL*; we managed to secure cheap rental fees for the venue because they wanted to support what was left of our community. However, we

---

8   https://twitter.com/kevinkaywho/status/972263525279178752
9   Check out the match here: https://www.youtube.com/watch?v=5EGHUMTXRmg

eventually stopped having monthly tournaments, and now we could only compete at the next Kawaii Kon. I didn't mind, as my studies were getting much more rigorous with senior level engineering classes and projects.

2013 was the first year where I wasn't able to attend Kawaii Kon due to having a major exam the following Monday. That year, everyone questioned my absence on Facebook. Why would I miss out on the tradition? There weren't going to be any other tournaments. Was I sure that I wanted to miss out on this? In the end, I regretted not showing up only because the exam turned out to be pretty easy despite being a large portion of our grade, and I got an almost-perfect score. While I was living in regret for the next day or two, I still loved how much I meant to the community. Despite the lack of events, I still had a belonging that I could always fall back on. The Kawaii Kon tournament itself still turned out great regardless of the lack of monthlies, with just as many entrants and with DEHF keeping his crown.

2014 was the final year for Brawl, as Smash 4 was coming out in the upcoming fall. In Kawaii Kon's doubles tournament, I had paired with Candi and her Falco, as she started attending tournaments after that birthday evening. We ended up placing third, the first time either of us scored money from a Kawaii Kon tournament. DarkMusician congratulated us as he remembered seeing our improvement over the years, despite the lack of monthlies. I even managed to beat Tita and Anteh one final time (though this was Candi's first time) in a two-versus-one situation, where I had only one stock left and they had a total of three stocks remaining. The comeback was amazing and DarkMusician also congratulated me on a well-deserved win. In singles, I had placed 13th out of about 50 entrants, my highest placing at Kawaii Kon yet. Unsurprisingly, DEHF took first. There was no stopping him.

In the late summer of 2014, Brawl made one final resurrection as a new event came up on the island: *Gamer Expo HI*. This was likely to bring in even more Smash fans than Kawaii Kon due to actually being a gaming event rather than an anime convention. DEHF was flown down here once more to leave a lasting statement. While this tournament held the same results, with me placing 13th and DEHF first, it brought in plenty of Smash players who were more than looking forward to the inevitable Smash 4 tournaments to come.

Super Smash Bros. Brawl was a fun ride while it lasted. After four years of competing in Brawl tournaments and seeing how far I had come, I was satisfied with how this chapter of my Smash career was about to close. Coincidentally, I was just about to graduate from college at the same time in Fall 2014 with a near 4.0 in my final semester, the highest I had ever obtained in my college career. I was about to obtain two degrees: one in computer engineering, and one in art with a focus on graphic design. The timelines between my life and Smash were aligning so perfectly: Brawl was dying at the perfect time when I needed to spend the majority of my time studying, and Smash 4 was just released the month before my graduation. The future was looking bright, and I couldn't wait to see what was waiting ahead.

Chapter Four

Aloha Smash 4

In October 2014, Nintendo launched the long-awaited *Super Smash Bros. for Nintendo 3DS*. A Wii U version was planned to be released a month later as Nintendo knew that if both were released at the same time, the 3DS sales would be significantly lower. Between these two months, the Brawl veterans had created a public Hawaii Facebook group "Smash for the 3ds/WiiU Hawaii[1]" for this upcoming game. This was a fantastic opportunity for the scene to start anew.

Smash 4 instantly became the next big trend on campus, no matter how big gamers students were. Now that Smash was available on the go for the first time, people loved being able to play a few matches during breaks, after school, or even during class (not me though, I swear!). Before then, people would have to bring their own console, TV, and controllers to school, on top of finding an open outlet that wasn't occupied by phones and laptops. While this was doable, friends would usually have to coordinate in advance, and even then, they couldn't play

---

1   This was renamed to "Super Smash Bros Ultimate Hawaii" in the fall of 2018. Regardless, check us out! https://www.facebook.com/groups/672648416185974/

too long because of varied schedules so oftentimes, planning everything wasn't worthwhile except maybe on a Friday night. Now, all everyone had to do was bring in their own 3DS, a handheld so small it could fit in one's pocket, and within minutes they could either win with pride or hide in humiliation.

I met plenty of colleagues and played against them throughout that semester just because I would see two strangers playing together on their 3DS. Every single time I saw two people on their handheld during that month, they were playing Smash. I stumbled upon Smash players in almost every place: before the start of each class, the cafeteria, the student union, after meetings at work, and even at the gym when people played while cycling. (I admittedly unlocked characters while cycling myself. Four years later, I still shamelessly do this but with the Nintendo Switch!) The timing of the Smash 3DS release really was just perfect. Since the game was released before midterms started kicking in, Smash was the starter of new friendships to carry throughout the rest of the semester, and for me, the rest of my college career. I even ended up finding helpful study partners because of this game.

I had never entered any of the 3DS tournaments nor focused on becoming skilled in this game at that time due to my final semester workload, but I would, regardless, carry my 3DS around campus. Fortunately, my fundamental skills carried over from Brawl and still gave people a challenge anytime I did get into a match. Everyone would be amazed at how difficult it would be to beat me, especially given that my Brawl main, Donkey Kong, was considered to be the absolute worst character in this new game (though that doesn't say too much given how little people know about a new game).

People would bring up that fact all the time. The only place known to host a tier list at that time was a website called *EventHubs*[2], and while this was the only source of truth, people knew it was still inaccurate due to how the tiers were decided: anyone and everyone could vote on it. Regardless, the people I faced actually enjoyed losing to me when they did. Because my character was considered low-tier, they believed that my win was honest and well-deserved, requiring more skill than using easy tactics from a higher tiered character.

After a quick session of Smash, when the class was about to start or when someone would need to leave, I would introduce them to the Hawaii Smash group on Facebook. They would always join instantly, whether they played casually or wanted to get into the competitive scene. Getting the group to grow was initially a struggle, starting with a small base of only the Brawl veterans, but the more people spread the word both online and offline, the more potential for the group to grow viral, now carrying about 800 members at the time of writing. It even grew big enough to reach out to competitive players living on the outer islands, who for the first time ever flew out to the Kawaii Kon tournament in 2016.

At the end of the month on a Saturday evening, a new member of the Facebook group, "Nuzlo[3]," hosted an open-invite Smashfest at the famous Ala Moana Center, or simply Ala Moana. Since he didn't know many other Smash players, nor was he attending school to meet people, he decided to try to find people at the number one meet-up spot. I

---

2   http://www.eventhubs.com/tiers/ssb4/

3   His tag "Nuzlo" came from the community-made Pokémon ruleset, the "Nuzlocke Challenge." At the simplest level, throughout the Pokémon gameplay, if a Pokémon of yours is no longer able to battle, you can no longer use them for the rest of the game. http://bulbapedia.bulbagarden.net/wiki/Nuzlocke_Challenge

happened to have a community band concert performance[4] at the same place and time, so I decided to check out the Smashfest beforehand, leaving for the concert when I had to and then coming back right after. While showing up and meeting strangers in a Hawaiian dress shirt[5] with a French horn was a bit awkward for me, this was the best decision both Nuzlo and I made in our Smash career.

When I arrived at the Smashfest before I had to meet up for the concert, only one individual sat there playing by himself by a large pillar in the food court, despite me arriving about ten minutes late[6]. We were expecting at least six people to swing by having contacted them all online, and with the giant pillar, a popular food court restaurant, and little black foldable devices in our hands, we knew we couldn't be missed. Half an hour later, there were six of us playing Smash, but as soon as the sixth person arrived, I had to leave for the band concert. An hour later and the five of them were still at it. We continued playing for the rest of the night until the mall closed. I wasn't accustomed to going alone to a meetup with strangers, but after that evening I started to get comfortable to this concept, even outside of Smash. After all, it's the only way to get to know people if you move to a new city.

I was still using my Smash skills to my advantage of forming these new friendships—I had only lost about three games that entire night—but I started feeling more comfortable in befriending strangers in general, starting up conversations outside of Smash and relying less on my gaming skills to create deep, meaningful conversations. Maybe it was because

---

4   From 2012 to 2014, I was intermittently a part of the local *Honolulu Wind Ensemble*, where at that time my high school band teacher was also the band director of this community band. https://sites.google.com/site/honoluluwindensemble/

5   Better known as Aloha shirt in Hawaii.

6   In Hawaii, this is known as "staying on Hawaiian time." http://www.urbandictionary.com/define.php?term=Hawaiian%20Time

I already knew they were Smashers, but even before playing against them I felt comfortable in making small talk, asking about what they're studying in school, what they do, etc. I had never been able to do so easily before as a shy introvert.

Since this pillar where we played provided a few outlets, we as a new group of friends would say to meet up at the "Pillar of Charge" for future meet-ups. I loved feeling that tiny pinch of rapport when I used or heard a term known among the few of us. I knew then that I'd become a part of a new group or community, however small. However cool (or lame) of a name it was, we had only met up once more here before the Wii U version came out the week before Thanksgiving[7]. Once the Wii U version was out, nobody would ever touch their 3DS anymore. Smashfests were going to happen at each other's homes, or at other public venues that provided monitors. Despite restricting where people could play, everyone preferred a larger screen and playing with a controller that actually had a control stick instead of a circle pad.

With these upcoming Smashfests, Nuzlo decided to make us an official crew called "Hold it Down!" or "HiD" for short, and I decided to join in because, well, why not? The motivation for that crew name was simple: everyone knew that GSM was the best crew on the island, and Nuzlo wanted another crew to give them a challenge, to hold their own, to hold it down.

Super Smash Bros. for Wii U, or "Smash 4" (nobody refers Smash 4 to the 3DS despite it being effectively the same game), came out on the Friday before Thanksgiving. Immediately, the next day, DarkMusician hosted a tournament celebrating its release. Although he hosted a 3DS tournament before this one and it attracted a nice 32 entrants, this Wii

---

7   After Thanksgiving, the mall decided to cover the outlets anyway so nobody could use them! We weren't going to play on these 3DS's anymore thanks to the Wii U version, but still how unfortunate.

U release tournament brought in over 40 entrants, a number we could only dream of for a monthly Brawl tournament. Fortunately, instead of the tiny computer store Brawl had near its end, we had a much larger card shop to share—you could probably fit about a hundred people there. Since I hadn't entered the former 3DS tournament, I was more astonished than others in seeing how many new faces there were, including the HiD people. This was an exciting time for me not because of how I'd place in this tournament but because I was curious about how the newcomers approached this tournament. Flashbacks came back to when I went to my first tournament years ago. I remembered just how much I wanted to perform well in the tournament and how I wanted to fit in with the community. As I passed by each individual, I often wondered, *How much do they like this new scene? How much does this game mean to them? Are they here to stay?* Only time could tell.

In terms of results, I frankly hadn't performed that badly in a while. Most of the entrants had allegedly stayed up late the night before, getting accustomed to the differences between the 3DS and the Wii U, but I was touching the GameCube controller (the Smash controller of choice, despite it being over a decade old) for the first time since Brawl. Everyone wanted to be the first to place first, as they all wanted to leave a fantastic first impression on the community. Unfortunately for me, there was no way I would even get close. My priorities simply weren't in Smash at that point in time, and given that I was less than a month away from graduating, I was more than fine with that.

On the same day, HiD challenged GSM to a crew battle, the first time an official crew battle had ever happened in the Hawaii Smash community. Crew battles are such an interesting concept. They originated from Japanese 2D fighting games decades ago but were popularized in Melee back in 2004. In this format, an equal number of players from each team take turns fighting one-on-one. The winner of the match carries their remaining stock count to the next match by intentionally jumping off the stage at the beginning, whereas the other team sends out a new player with a full stock count. The crews continue this until one crew loses all of their players, in which the other crew is declared as the winner.[8]

This crew battle was a 6-on-6 match with the original six people from HiD's Pillar of Charge, and GSM ended up winning with six out of twelve stocks to spare (in this crew battle, and in most Smash 4 tournaments, each player only had two stocks). Frankly, everyone expected GSM to win, but the camaraderie among all of the community members had never felt more united. This was truly the perfect way to start this new scene, to welcome this new generation of players. We may have formed a bit of a dichotomy by forming a second crew, but the rivalry between the crews gave the Smash community a sense of challenge, belonging, and desire to become the best players we could be.

While the game and that tournament day were as exciting as a monthly could ever be, I didn't touch Smash for a while until graduation day. School decided to take over with its final exams and senior project deadlines coming up. With that, I wanted Smash to be the first thing I did after graduation, so I invited HiD and all my other Smash friends to a Smashfest at my place that afternoon. Everything seemed perfect with having accomplished the biggest achievement of my life yet, unwinding with my favorite hobby surrounded by friends both old and new, and having no worries on my mind for what's to come. I even had an in-person job interview in California lined up the upcoming month after having passed multiple phone interviews, so everything was absolutely smooth sailing.

---

8   http://www.ssbwiki.com/Crew_battle

The next day was tournament day, and HiD felt more prepared than ever after practicing the day before. I had actually placed the highest ever in my Smash career, placing third out of about 40 entrants, and my crewmates performed better than the last time as well. My brain was on a natural high that weekend, with achievements coming in left and right. What could stop me?

On the same day, I had challenged a new-generation Smasher to a money match, or a cash battle. A money match is a set agreed on by each player with cash on the line, typically applying the same rules as during a tournament. With money on the line and the simulation of competing in a tournament, unless we didn't care about throwing away our money, the pressure would be just as great if not greater than an actual tournament set. The winner would be rewarded with not only cash but also pride.[9]

This was an exciting event that DarkMusician recorded and commentated, not only because money matches never happened in our local community but also because this Smash player, "Atmosfear," also used Donkey Kong. While he was never a part of the Brawl competitive scene, I challenged him because he had actually placed higher than me in the previous tournament, so it still seemed like a fair match. This was a close set going to last-stock last-hit, but in the end, I humbly lost and gave him the $5 he deserved. People considered the match to be an upset[10], but I didn't mind since upsets made everything more interesting. Because of that set, I was no longer considered the best Donkey Kong on the island, but I was sure to change that in the near future. Later did we know, I ended up having to play him in the two tournaments

9   http://www.ssbwiki.com/money_match

10   The term "upset" is referred to when an unexpected result occurs, or when the player known to be the better gamer loses. This term is used not only in Smash but also in all forms of competition, even in sports.

immediately following this one, but I scored convincing wins against him both times.

Everything was looking to be so perfect. Everyone enjoyed Smash 4 a lot more than Brawl, bringing in many more players to the competitive scene, both in Hawaii and worldwide. I was finally out of school, and my only priority during the immediate months after college was studying up on programming interview books (and even though I treated this studying as a full-time job, I still had plenty of time on the weekends and evenings while my brain digested that information), so I was able to make bettering my Smash skills a priority. Resources were more than available for me to improve: an active Facebook group for analysis and discussion, friends who were just as dedicated to becoming great players, and even a crew for regular practice. Within the training grounds of our crew, HiD was also recruiting players so that we'd have a greater variety when practicing. Nuzlo made sure that the people he recruited were both ambitious with potential and also well-rounded people with amicable personalities.

HiD started hosting weekly Smashfests on Sundays at a LAN center called PC Gamerz. For only $5 per session, we could play there for the entire day, coming in and out as we pleased. I always looked forward to and treasured those days, not only for regular improvement but for a shot of a social life after college and outside of college friends, something that many new grads claim to have difficulty in especially since they would never realize that they would have that problem. We would arrive at around 11 A.M. and would just keep playing for hours, sometimes until 11 P.M., sometimes until 3 A.M., really until the last person wanted to leave or when the venue closed at 4 A.M., given they didn't have any responsibilities to tend to the following day. Sometimes we would skip out on dinner because our only hunger was for improvement, and other times we would eat out together at the restaurants next door. In our eyes, we didn't mind binging out on gaming for such extensive hours as long as it wasn't multiple times a week. Everyone in our crew was aware of life balance and moderation. On Sundays, life was stress-free, and with this sense of belonging within a group of people who shared the same passion, life was pretty great.

* * *

I was playing well in the monthly tournaments, consistently placing top 12 out of at least 30. HiD kept meeting up and playing regularly on the weekends whenever a tournament wasn't scheduled. Even GSM started showing up to PC Gamerz, and all the regulars would meet up at every Smashfest. I was leveling up at an insane speed compared to the Brawl days, and I was having much more fun with the game, thanks to all the people sharing this ambition. While the prior days of playing with FTL, Tita, and Anteh were great, I was limited in both my playtime due to school as well as my skill cap since I was learning how to win against their playstyles instead of how to improve my fundamental skills. (Unfortunately, the three of them don't play the game anymore.) To paint a clearer picture, for example in Chess, the one opponent you always play might constantly miss the fact that you're using your pawns as bait, so you abuse those pawns as often as possible. You're not necessarily becoming a better Chess player; you're just becoming comfortable against that specific opponent. In one-versus-one competition, it is imperative to practice against as many people as possible, as you'll need to be comfortable in facing any situation in the long haul.

With how often everyone was meeting up, the community resembled a closely-knit family, with both the Brawl veterans and the newer Smash 4 players coming together. While back in the Brawl days, we would improve in our cliques, now the entire community would work together to become the best they can be. The tournament regulars were always open to meeting new people, whether in another tournament or at PC Gamerz and when they did, they made sure that the newcomer felt welcomed and comfortable. You could see the frustration in the newcomers' faces when they got beaten by the veterans, but the veterans kept the newcomers coming through positive reinforcement. They would talk about how everyone started off by losing, they would give the newbies tips for improvement after every match, and they just loved keeping the community open for anyone to join in. The *aloha* in the Hawaii Smash community was and will forever be real.

Smash aside, in March, I was confirmed for the job! After my interview in January, I was told two weeks later that they would go through a background check and that I would need to fill out several forms since this was a government position. The process took a bit more than a month, and by the beginning of March, I received the official offer.

Once again the timelines would align for me perfectly, as March was also the month of none other than Kawaii Kon. The event would be held at the end of the month, and thus I declared my starting date to be the week after. The timing of the offer was actually perfect since a month was just enough for me to get ready to move out, hang out with my friends and family one last time, and get acclimated to a new life in California, specifically San Diego.

In the tournament, before I was offered the job, DarkMusician started announcing the line-up for the special guests to arrive for Kawaii Kon. This time, he had four special guests planned, with majority of the funds coming out of his own pocket (with the help of donation funds throughout previous tournaments). In comparison to bringing in only DEHF every year, this news got everyone excited for what's to come. The first and only guest he mentioned that day was the only one

I needed to hear: "DKwill."

The crowd went wild as DarkMusician announced his name, and everyone kept coming up to me throughout the day on my thoughts of his special appearance. You could probably guess why given his gamer tag. Given the fact that Donkey Kong was considered a low-to-mid-tier character (no longer the worst character in the game), nobody would have ever expected his name, especially since DKwill was coming all the way from New York. He even made great use of Donkey Kong back in Brawl (even then considered mid-tier), winning against the pros who used top-tier characters in a game where characters that weren't considered top-tier did not stand a chance among the upper echelon of players. DKwill claimed a niche spot on the list of pro Smash players as indisputably the best Donkey Kong in the world, and he claimed spot number 39 on the 2014 Brawl rankings. I had tried to keep an outward calm presence throughout the day, especially since everyone including DarkMusician was looking at me when he announced the news, but my mind was exploding with glee just like any fanboy would.

Throughout the upcoming month, all I did was study up YouTube videos of DKwill's tournament matches. While he didn't win all of them, the fact that he could fare with the top tiers was inspiring. Every time I asked the crew what I would do differently from him, everyone would respond "Not much," or "Honestly you do the same things that he does" After comparing my recorded matches to his gameplay, I couldn't help but agree—it wasn't much different. My confidence kept rising every time I heard these repeating comments throughout the month. Everyone believed that if any Donkey Kong in the world could take him out in the tournament, it would be me.

On his first day in Hawaii, we both put $50 on the table. $100 sat proudly next to the console, waiting for the best Donkey Kong player of the day. Maybe DKwill was the best Donkey Kong player, but I *am* Donkey Kong. It was in my tag: "I, DK."A first-to-five money match (whoever wins five games first wins) was about to commence, and the entire Smash community couldn't wait for it to begin.

When I first walked into the venue on the Tuesday afternoon before Kawaii Kon for a casual "meet and play," DarkMusician eagerly introduced me to the world-famous Donkey Kong player. Despite DKwill's status, he was as amicable as he was talented. You could effortlessly tell that he loved meeting new people, let alone fellow Donkey Kong mains. He didn't treat his fans as fans but as new friends. His love for the game and the friends that came with it was pure, and witnessing this from such a high-level player was awe-inspiring.

He absolutely loved the fact that I challenged him at such a high stake, and we both knew that I was challenging him for that much not because I thought it was going to be easy but as a way to bring more excitement into the game we love. Was it a reckless idea, coming from a 22-year-old? Frankly, yes, yes it was. But given my situation, I couldn't help it! It was my final week in Hawaii, it was my one chance to face the best Donkey Kong in the world, I was about to get my first engineering paycheck, etc. Even if I lost, it would have been a great way to support my favorite player. Although financially it was not the greatest idea, the experience was more than priceless.

As we discussed the beginning of our first-to-five set, he asked me, "Do you have any stage preferences? We're going to have a lot of games to play!" I smiled and responded, "Anywhere but FD," short for the stage called "Final Destination." This stage consisted of a single, wide stage with absolutely zero other stage elements. All other stages contained at least one smaller floating platform above the main stage, and Donkey Kong's strengths shined considerably with more platforms. DKwill knew this, and from the immediate smile, it was clear that we shared an instant connection. Not even the sets between Atmosfear and me nor between So Desu and me exhibited a rapport so transparent.

Five games later... let's not talk about that.

While DKwill didn't lose a single game, I did take several stocks off him. And money aside, he loved every moment of it. He loved the confidence in someone challenging him with such a high stake, compared to many others who money matched him $5 just to say that they've tried. He loved my shared enthusiasm for the character. He even claimed that playing against me felt almost ethereal because a lot of my decision making was similar to his, recalling a lot of thoughts akin to "I would've done that too!" and making difficult decisions on the spot because he had to counter his own strategies. Out of all the Donkey Kongs, he played against throughout the country, he stated that mine was at a level he had not faced in quite a long time, if not ever.

Throughout the set, stock after stock, game after game, I was downloading all of DKwill's techniques. How did he get into this advantageous position and net the first stock before I did? What did he do to punish this option? How did he avoid getting hit, or losing a stock, to my options? How was he simply playing so fast, and how was he making such quick decisions? I had been asking myself these questions minute after minute while barely being able to keep up with his somehow safe yet aggressive playstyle. Even after the set, he pointed out a few obvious flaws that I could have avoided, knowing that I was searching for improvement. After all, with losses come not failures, but great lessons to learn from.

After that set, all I wanted to do was learn from DKwill. Despite being such an erudite student in academia, I never had the desire to take in so much so quickly. During that week, I had the best resource to take advantage of, and with that paired with my immediate loss, the passion to grow as a Smasher had never felt stronger. Throughout the next two to three hours, all I did was sit behind him and observe his decision making as he played out more money matches against the rest of Hawaii. Oftentimes, simply observing was enough when I could answer my own questions, but once in a while, I would ask why he did a particular move or made a specific decision. He clearly loved answering these types of questions, especially for his given character. *Instead of using your shield, block the attack with your own attack. Instead of running and shielding to get through projectiles, walk and jab them. Don't be afraid to go deep off the stage—DK can make it back* (despite the character being known for having lackluster options to recover[11] back onto the stage). Fortunately, Hawaii was blessed with great character diversity, so on top of learning the fundamentals of Donkey Kong himself, I was also internalizing what decisions to make against a wide variety of opponents. Normally I would rush out to play more games against my friends—after all, as studies show we learn best by doing right?—but I knew I had to make use of his presence while he was here. While neither DKwill nor I explicitly said this, we both knew he became my mentor for the day.

Once I started playing again later that day, my wins were proving that my brain had internalized everything. I was trying to implement all the tips I had gathered throughout the day, and despite feeling uncomfortable with getting rid of old habits and decisions, all of the new tricks were working. I remember when I was on a friendly station with three others, including two of the top ten Hawaii players plus DKwill himself. With multiple players on one setup, we would take turns (called "rotations") playing one-versus-one matches in a king-of-the-hill style where the

---

11   In Smash, recovery is the attempt to return onstage, either after being knocked off or by purposely falling off. The latter is done to hinder other opponents' recovery.

winner stays. Smashers usually play one game before rotating, as we did that day, but sometimes people play best-of-three sets to replicate tournament settings. I ended up continuously playing in that rotation for a solid half hour without dropping a game! It even took DKwill multiple attempts to knock me off my throne.

* * *

Kawaii Kon weekend finally came around, and it was time to prove what I learned. I felt like I was back in school with finals week just around the corner. I had studied and practiced all that I could that week, and it was now time to put everything to the test. Well... almost.

This three-day event always started off on Friday with a free-for-all event with items on, intended for anyone to jump in and have fun regardless of skill. This was actually my first time competing in this event, as I could never make it to the convention on Fridays due to school. While skill was still required to take the whole thing, for the most part, anything goes with items and with the possibility of three players ganging up on one. I highly recommend tournament organizers to host a side event like this once in a while. Everyone loves it, with both newer players having a greater chance of playing more matches in bracket as well as competitive players just taking a break from serious competition.

Saturday was a doubles tournament per usual, and this time I decided to pair up with Atmosfear, scaring everyone in bracket with not one but two Donkey Kongs. While this was a lot more competitive than free-for-all with zero luck involved (albeit just as chaotic), having a partner allowed having a greater margin of error and thus was generally more enjoyable, hence the event coming up before singles. Atmosfear and I placed within the top 12 out of about 40 teams, a new record for doubles entrants in Smash Hawaii history. Our first loss was to a team that included an out-of-state guest, and our second was against the top five players in the state, so overall we had a good run.

Sunday came around and everyone was ready to win. There were three other out-of-state players besides DKwill: DEHF who in Smash 4 now goes by "Larry Lurr" and uses Fox[12] instead of Falco, "Jtails" a Diddy Kong[13] player from New York City who currently lives in Central California, and "NinjaLink" a player from Brooklyn, New York, who wields many characters but in this tournament utilized Mega Man[14] the most. Ninety-two participants. Two crews. And the rest of the Hawaii Smash community. Everyone was warmed up from the past two days, if not the whole week, and people were ready to win it all. You could tell who was going to place high from the look on their faces. Some were there simply looking forward to a great time. Others were nervous. The rest—the out-of-state players and top Hawaii players—remained poised with nothing but the trophy in their sight.

I was fortunate to have DKwill around to coach me during sets whenever he was available, similar to having a coach in a boxing match. The rules for having a coach in Smash varies for each tournament, but

---

12   Fox from the *Star Fox* series is known to be one of the top ten characters in the game due to his incredible speed and combo potential, paired with a reflecting tool that denies all projectiles and forces ranged characters to play his game. On the other hand, his fast falling speed makes him more susceptible than others to combos, his recovery options are easily predictable and punishable, and his light weight makes him lose stocks earlier than usual.

13   Diddy Kong from the *Donkey Kong Country* series is a nimble character known for his strength with banana peels, an item that he can pull out at any time, with one banana in the game at a time. The banana peel can be thrown from a distance and hence is often safe to attack with, even if it misses. An opponent getting hit by the banana peel trips for a second, allowing Diddy Kong to follow up with a grab combo or any attack, racking up damage quickly. His weaknesses lie in being extremely vulnerable when he gets knocked off the stage, allowing opponents to take stocks early. People believe Diddy Kong to be one of the top ten best characters.

14   Mega Man is known to be a character whose strengths lie in keeping opponents away with his wide arsenal of projectiles and sheer power in his killing moves. His overall mobility is lackluster however, his weight allows him to fall into combos easily similarly to Fox, and characters who don't care about projectiles like Fox negate most of Mega Man's options.

nowadays as of 2018 coaches are generally not allowed in the middle of a match. At this place and time, however, players were allowed up to thirty seconds of coaching in between games during a set. Having a coach could change the pace of a match completely; as they could give you the immediate feedback you need but may not see for yourself after a game. Even the best players benefit from coaching. (The argument for banning coaching was that it required the right connections at the perfect place and time, plus it discouraged players from adapting on their own. This trumped over the benefit of coaching which mostly created more interesting matches, as a player tries to counteract what their opponent's coach may have told them).

After multiple close matches, my run finished as I placed 13th out of 92 players, losing to the one and only Larry Lurr who won the tournament, as well as one of the best Hawaii players "Dren," a Yoshi[15] player in the GSM crew who took 7th and also had the closest games with the out-of-state players. I remember thinking at the moment, *I could live with this—the 13th place was well deserved.* Of course, I wanted more, but during that weekend there was nothing more I could do. DKwill's training and advice throughout the day was essential to my placing, and I couldn't feel more fortunate for his tutelage over the past week. Now, the next step was to take my play just as far on my own. I learned how to learn, indisputably one of the most paramount skills to acquire in life.

At the end of the convention and tournament, my crew and I

---

15   Yoshi from the *Super Mario* series (recognized as its own franchise, the *Yoshi's Island* universe, in the Smash series) takes pride in his amazing aerial mobility paired with good strength and overall speed. He also has a versatile projectile that can be difficult to get past. He also has options to getting out of combos more easily than other characters, including an aerial attack that comes out immediately and a jump in mid-air that grants him limited anti-flinching armor, or *heavy armor*, while he is jumping. (*Super armor* would allow receiving unlimited damage in a period of time.) His slower defensive options however keep him from getting higher than top twenty on the tier list.

gathered together with DKwill for a farewell photo, since this was my last Hawaii tournament before heading out to California. Friends were starting to bring out small gifts: leis, snacks, even a drawing of Donkey Kong saying "Hawaii's best Donkey Kong! Good luck in Cali!" As we gathered together, Nuzlo came through with an unusually large bag...

"Surprise!"

And what a surprise it was—a brand new Wii U! Signed by the entire Hawaii Smash community and the out-of-state players, and contributed by players both in and outside of our crew. To this day it remains the best gift I have ever received, not only for its price tag and how useful it would be for me but because of its significance. People were going to miss me, my Donkey Kong, my helping of the community, the Smashfests, the tournaments, the hangouts outside of Smash, the teaching out-of-state players how to use chopsticks at a Korean bar called "Cafe Duck Butt," the... late night panels at the anime convention the night before the singles tournament...[16] and every other memory we had shared, whether it was the past five years or only the past five days. Of course, I would miss them the same and still do today.

Every time I come back to visit Hawaii, the Smash community is the one thing I miss the most. There is something special about the Smash community that I just can't pinpoint. Maybe it's the shared immense love and dedication to that one video game. Maybe it's the fact that we're so busy playing the game that there's rarely any drama that happens in real life. Maybe it's the tournaments and Smashfests that decide for us what we plan to do and when to meet up.

I think it's the fact that this isn't just a hobby, but also a goal that we're all working towards, trying to be the best Smash player we could be, surpassing our potential every day. We're not just a group of friends

---

16   Disgusting, but an oddly amazing social activity.

socializing, eating out, and having a good conversation. We're human beings doing what human beings do to give their lives meaning: striving toward an ultimate goal, together.

The most significant people worth talking about are always those who have accomplished great achievements in their lives, whether their success comes from their creation of the latest technology, their advances on society, or whatever it may be. As video gamers, we're really trying to do the same thing, just with the video game as our tool of choice. We're all meant to achieve great things, and as a Smash community, that's all we're really trying to do, one game at a time.

Chapter Five

America's Finest City

In April 2015, I had moved out to the wonderful county of San Diego, probably the closest you could get to Hawaii both literally in distance as well as figuratively in the beaches and sunshine. I knew no one here, and here I was trying to start my software engineering career by jumping onto a government project that involved satellite networks. Oh. I still can't believe the company trusted a group of new grads to tackle such a prestigious project.

I did have one thing going for me moving here, however, and by now we all know what that is. While I had picked a good location for work, Southern California was also known to be one of the strongest Smash regions in the nation. The sheer size of the Los Angeles, San Diego, and Orange counties make an amazing amalgamation of skill and knowledge that is unmatched. The best Smash 4 player in the world "ZeRo" used to reside in Los Angeles for a great period of time at the beginning of Smash 4's lifespan, and one of the top Melee players in the world "Mango" (or "Mang0") also lives in the Los Angeles County. You'll also find many esports teams and companies in Southern California. Varying esports teams here include Team SoloMid, Counter Logic Gaming, and Immortals, all who sponsor the top 20 Smash 4 players. Gaming companies here include Riot Games (publisher for *League of Legends*), Blizzard Entertainment (for *Overwatch*, *Hearthstone*, and more), and Twitch (the live streaming video platform intended primarily for esports). There was a lot going on here and I couldn't wait to be a part of it all.

Similar to the Hawaii Smash Facebook group, I searched for the Southern California (or SoCal) Facebook group to see where I could find the local scene. Lo and behold, the group was huge with about three thousand members! (As of July 2018, it sits at triple the numbers at nine thousand.) By happenstance, I also found a separate San Diego Smash Facebook group, which sat at a more tangible size of three hundred (about 2,000 at time of writing). I welcomed myself on the group page, but unfortunately, the post caught the attention of only one other person. Maybe the scene was more welcoming, or more active, in person?

Throughout my beginning weeks in the new city, I was keeping an eye out on the group page, not going out to any events because of settling in with work and exploring the city on the weekends. Unfortunately, it seemed like there weren't any Smashers in any nearby cities, let alone any tournaments. The closest and most popular tournament was on Thursday nights and about a 40-minute drive from my home since I lived in the northern part of the county, and 40 minutes felt disgustingly long for this kid from Hawaii where a drive across the island would take an hour. In addition, I wasn't planning on purchasing a car yet, wanting to build up my funds first before I immediately added another bill to account for, and getting to the venue by public transportation from work was literally impossible on weeknights. (Let's not even talk about the $40 Uber ride!) Smash life was looking rather grim, but it was such a huge passion for me that I was going to make it work no matter what. I live in Southern California, where the greatest players of Smash reside, so of course, it's going to work, right? In the meantime, I would get my training in by playing online with my new Wii U against my Hawaii friends, mostly as a way to keep in touch. One of my friends had even moved to Peru for the year for an internship, and despite sharing an Internet connection of over 4,000 miles with a developing country in a different continent, I would still play games with him fairly often just because of how much we could make fun of the Peruvian lag. We suffered together as we watched our inputs come out after a full two-second delay, and we waited for the game to buffer more often than not.

Smash was looking as bright as San Diego itself when I found out someone was about to host a tournament on a weekend near the end of my first month here. Unfortunately, it was even farther than the weekly, almost an hour away by car, almost three full hours by public transportation. I did have the fortune of getting a ride from a fellow community member, despite not having met him before. He went by the tag "Fezz" and gave me a pleasant welcome to the community, especially with his ride offer and his driving out in the opposite direction just to help a stranger out. We turned out to be around the same age and related rather well, as he was just about to graduate from college and join the world of adulthood soon. Even today he still shows great hospitality towards the San Diego Smash community and I will always be grateful for his efforts and respect.

The tournament itself was a rather small event with only sixteen people in a Smash player's garage, despite being close to downtown on a Saturday. Having Fezz around was comforting as I had at least one person to talk to throughout the event. He pointed out to me the guys to watch out for as they walked in, the power ranked guys or PR for short. Each region would have an official power ranking list of usually ten of the top players, determined every two to three months by a few panelists within the region who would bring up the statistics of every single local tournament's results and figure things out from there. San Diego was large enough of a county to have its own power ranking of ten players, while the entirety of Southern California would include its top twenty players. Hawaii never had a power ranking list until just a few months after I moved out. I may or may not have the immediate skill to get on that list, but I knew I had the determination to get there eventually. I knew that outside of my career, this would be the number one goal.

As I walked into the garage, immediately I could sense a conflicting dichotomy in the scene, at least for that day. There was a clear division between the power ranked Smashers and the rest of the players there, not only in skill but also in the sense of community. It felt as if there were two completely separate cliques despite sharing the same hobby and vicinity. Not one person said a word to another in the other group, not even a simple hello, despite the small size of the venue. This was nothing like how it was in Hawaii, where everyone prioritized getting along with one another over anything else.

Frankly, the skill gap was just as wide as the geniality between these cliques of Smashers. Before the tournament started, I was playing friendlies with most of the non-ranked players, and they were shockingly easy to beat. My Donkey Kong was able to take away everyone's stocks without taking much damage myself. Everyone was starting to talk about me, ranging from "He's so good even as a Donkey Kong!" to "I think we finally have someone who can take down the PR!" Meanwhile, the PR members that were there would keep talking quietly among themselves.

Strangers befriending me because of my skill was nothing new, but that did help me acclimate to the San Diego Smash community, and things were finally starting to look up. They loved how I would give them tips after each friendly match, receiving comments from them including "No one ever helps the lesser guys, I really appreciate it" and "Thank you so, so much!" The divide was evidently real. I always believed that there should be some balance between teaching one another and having one learn for themselves, but the former didn't seem to be a thing here.

In the tournament itself, I ended up losing all my games, and rather quickly as well. One loss was to the highest-ranked player in San Diego at that time, "Ito" who was also nationally well-known for innovating the character Meta Knight[1] (as well as later being the Nintendo World Championships 2017[2] winner), and another loss was to number 4 on the San Diego power ranking at that time. The talent of those players was admitted far greater than those in Hawaii. This tournament gave me an awakening in realizing what Southern California and the world of competitive Smash truly had to offer. I still had a long way to go.

The second tournament I entered in San Diego was not until two months later on a Saturday in June, an event that hosted almost a hundred entrants in a card shop as big as the one in Hawaii. Unfortunately, getting there required over two hours by public transportation, but since this was on the weekend I didn't mind making it work (I would just plop into my world of books during these long trips). Lots of people whom I met from my first tournament recognized me there, welcoming me back to the scene. I also started befriending many of the regulars in the

---

1   Meta Knight from the *Kirby* series is known to be one of the top fifteen characters in the game due to his quick ranged attacks and combos that allow early kills, paired with recovery options that are difficult to punish. He is however susceptible to getting blocked out by projectiles, and is also light-weight and so is susceptible to dying earlier.

2   The *Nintendo World Championship* is a video game competition series hosted by the company of Nintendo itself. Qualifying rounds took place in various cities throughout the US, and few would make it to the final round where competitors would face off playing Nintendo games that haven't even been released yet. https://nwc.nintendo.com/

scene after they recognized me for my play and saw me placing pretty well. Frankly, I still had some a mix of shyness and anxiety in going up to a stranger and saying hi, and thus I kept using my skill as my clutch for socializing and having people approach me instead.

My first match that day was against a third power-ranked player, and the TO decided to put us on the main stage, where a projector connected to the setup for everyone to watch. At that time, I was still unfamiliar with the power ranking list and hence I had no idea, but after a few seconds into our match, I could tell that this match was going to be difficult. He had a heavy bait-and-punish playstyle, not committing to any attacks until I tried getting in and messing up, yet I was aware of his intentions. With that, the match lasted quite long, but somehow I barely won that set. I extended out my hand for a handshake, a typical tournament standard after each match (or at least a fist bump), especially since I believed it was a well-played set from the both of us. Unfortunately, he shook his head instead of my hand while walking away and talking to his friends about the loss. Shrugging it off, I walked away from the projector to see people immediately approaching me. They would talk about how Donkey Kong was never used here, how the guy I played was a ranked player and little things here and there that made the win exciting.

I continued on with my bracket and won about five matches, all who were much easier than my first win. While one was too upset to say a word after he lost, I was more than willing to keep in touch with the others after some fun games. Eventually, I met another power-ranked player where, although it was as intense and close as the first match of the day, my opponent emerged as the victor this time. He was the first power-ranked player I met who seemed quite amicable toward unranked players. Our match was as close as one could get: game three, last stock, last hit, in a best-of-three match. He admitted that we were practically at the same skill level, but he ended up making a few more correct guesses that were just enough to win the match. Regardless of the results, he enjoyed the match and said it'd be great to play against me again, which was quite pleasant to hear after everything I've seen in San Diego thus far.

Unfortunately, I did not survive a single round in my loser's bracket. The tournament organizer realized that since we were running out of time, he suddenly changed the rules to make all loser's matches from then on a best-of-one match, giving little time to adapt to the opponent's playstyle and allowing little to no forgiveness to unfortunate mistakes. In my case, I held a significant lead the entire game but lost my last stock in only two hits as I failed to recover via a misinput, giving him the "set." I ended up winning 9th place out of over 90 players, leaving unsatisfied knowing that I deserved higher if it weren't for the sudden change of rules. Even my opponent admitted that he did not deserve that win. Placings aside, I was more interested in what my strengths and weaknesses were, and this was just one tournament out of many more to come. More importantly to me, however, I wanted to leave the greatest impression on this community since first impressions really do mean everything. I left the venue with unexpected friendships, many whom I still talk to today while having the fortune of getting a 40-minute drive back home from a new friend when I was planning on catching two hours of public transportation back.

Unfortunately, there weren't any more weekend tournaments for a long time. I was able to attend only two or three of the Thursday weekly tournaments for the year plus three or four larger-scale tournaments thanks to generous carpools. Regardless, I knew I needed to make each tournament count, both with improving my skills as a player and with networking with as many people as I could. After that tournament, I swore myself to a new rule I would adhere by, no matter what, inside and outside of Smash:

Give equal attention and respect to everyone you meet in life. Don't put anyone on a pedestal, and don't put down anyone below you. Despite the variance in skill level, we all share the same emotions of victory and defeat, of partaking in the path of everlasting improvement. At the most fundamental level, we're all human beings who simply want to make the most of what life has to offer.

From my impressions on the San Diego Smash community thus far, it seemed that I could only be respected both as a player and as an individual if and only if I were a skilled player. I was starting to think that Hawaii was an exception to this rule and I was fortunate to have grown up in such a welcoming Smash community that defined the meaning of aloha. Top players in this new community didn't necessarily disrespect lesser players; they were simply indifferent, which isn't bad per se. It made sense from a biological perspective, where people tend to lean toward others whom they can benefit from; in Smash this would be for example a training partner, and in school for example that could be a new study partner or someone to work with on a school project. I still wanted to reject that social norm, however, even if it meant exerting more of my own time and energy for little to no gain in skill—for the sake of making our lives better, one smile at a time. From that day on, I wanted to unify the dichotomies of the top and lesser players by giving each member of the community the respect they deserve as humans beings. To higher-skilled players, I would thank them for their time and patience and in return try to give them specific tips on playing against my character since Donkey Kong was so rare. To lower-skilled players, I would ask after a match if they would like some quick advice (because forcing advice onto someone may make them think "ugh, he thinks he's that great," or they may simply be too upset from losing) and then give them a tip or two so they leave the tournament with something to think about, on top of an open invite to play online later to help them out. I frankly didn't care for this meritocratic environment, wishing I could share with this community the aloha I grew up within Hawaii.

I also swore to treat each person I met outside of Smash the same way, from a smiling hello on the street, to a fellow pedestrian, to asking the cashier at the grocery store how their day was. It may seem at first that you have nothing to gain by putting in that much effort, but the smile on a new acquaintance's face really should be more than enough of a reward, even if it's only beneficial in that given moment. If not, it makes a great reminder that we are simply trying to live in this world, trying to make it as human beings. This really doesn't take that much effort when you practice it regularly either and that's coming from me of all introverts. We all have the power to make someone's day, so let's make the most of it. After all, what's there to lose?

* * *

Today, I am immensely grateful for the friendships I have made here in sunny San Diego, despite having a rougher start than I expected. I've joined friends in rides to multiple tournaments, from a national in Ontario to an international tournament all the way up north in Oakland, to the largest fighting game tournament in the world in Las Vegas. Few friends were dedicated to the grind of improvement as we would carpool together on weeknights to Los Angeles every single week, driving over two hours one way just to hone our craft with the best of Southern California, leaving right after work and coming back at 1 A.M. There were even a few times where I flew with friends across the country just to compete. I'm so fortunate to have friends who are just as passionate about this game as I am, if not more.

Even locally within San Diego, many were willing to grind with me in matches I was uncomfortable with, teaching me all about beating specific characters, regardless of whether they were better or worse than me. We played together, shared stories inside and outside of Smash, ate out at Denny's (the one restaurant open at 3 A.M.) and Raising Cane's (the late-night chicken-finger fuel of practically all Smash players), and let ourselves vulnerable by confiding in each other our fears of failures to become our best. The community had fortunately been slowly closing the divide I mentioned earlier, as a result of both intentional effort and natural growth of the scene. So many of my non-Smash friends are envious of this social life outside of work since we have all learned first-hand (for those of us who are no longer in school) just how difficult making friends can be once we graduate. For this, I would always be grateful for being able to play the game I love with welcoming people wherever I am—literally anywhere.

In 2016, people starting asking on the Facebook group if there is a scene in my city far up north in the county. Everyone would respond "regrettably, no" or "I wish!" I decided to pay it forward by hosting my own gatherings at my place on a weekly basis, hoping to bring in some activity. I've made even closer friends due to sheer proximity thanks to these gatherings. While these gatherings were made up of only four to eight people, everybody always looked forward to coming by on these nights. Not only did they appreciate how the gathering was within the city, but they also respected how it was free to come to and just play instead of spending $10 at a tournament. The gatherings also showed how tiny this city is. I once gave my address to a guy interested in stopping by only to get the response "How do you know my address?!?" and finding out that he lived literally in the apartment below me. I discovered another friend who lived just two miles away and happened to work at the same company as I do, also as a recent graduate in software engineering, though we had never seen each other at work before. A college student was inspired to start his own Smash club at his university after attending these gatherings. Another guy has been so devoted to becoming better that he had asked me to train privately with him on top of those gatherings, and I was pleased to not only help him as a player but to also see his attitude change with his improvement and mindset in life. He would slowly change the way he spoke, from impossibility to unknown possible. "It's impossible to beat this!" would instead become "How do you get around this move?" A group of four brothers decided to start a weekly tournament series in partnership with a card shop in the adjacent city just four miles away—turns out three of them are members of the rock band CHON, and the next minute I realized that my sparring partners were rock band celebrities. Most importantly, I had a regular who zealously took an Uber ride each time tell me one evening "I really appreciate you hosting this every week, as it just takes me away from my troubles every time," on top of seeing a massive improvement over just a few weeks.

Even though this may only affect a few individuals, the impact left on each individual was more than significant in my eyes. The most amazing aspect of giving is this chain reaction that develops from one person's decision. Those whom I have helped are giving advice to newer players, especially with empathy when they realize that the struggles the newer players face are parallel to experiences the better players had gone through just a few weeks ago. Others are starting to host gatherings at their own homes, even if only one or two others would come by. Small actions, great impacts. The smallest acts of kindness can make the greatest difference, even through video games.

Chapter Six

From Basements to Ballrooms

Every year, thousands of fighting game enthusiasts travel from all around the world to compete, to spectate, to celebrate all that is fighting games. Where to? In a city you probably wouldn't expect: Las Vegas. Indeed, every summer these gamers come down to Sin City not for gambling, not for the nightlife, not for the live entertainment, but for *video games*. Nobody would have imagined ten years ago, let alone today, that over 10,000 gamers would gather in hotel ballrooms to celebrate video games, especially in the same building as where you can find alcohol-licensed casinos nonetheless.

The *Evolution Championship Series*, or *EVO* for short, is the most renowned fighting game event series in the world. It started back in 1996, initially called *Battle By the Bay* in Sunnyvale, California, with a 40-man bracket in *Super Street Fighter II Turbo* and *Street Fighter Alpha 2*. They later changed their name in 2002 and relocated to the Las Vegas strip in 2005, now hosting nine titles and over ten thousand participants annually. While this fighting game event is most recognized for its game of origin in the Street Fighter series, EVO also featured games from the series *Marvel vs. Capcom, Mortal Kombat, Guilty Gear, Killer Instinct, Tekken*, and more. The Smash series was later introduced to EVO back in 2007 with Melee, then with its new brethren Brawl replacing Melee in 2008.[1]

Neither game made a reappearance the next few years until 2013 when Melee made a return. EVO had selected seven out of nine games for the lineup that year, giving the community the opportunity to vote via donations on what game they wanted as the eighth game (with the ninth game being a last-minute addition, *Injustice: Gods Among Us*, with logistical support from its publisher Warner Bros). All processes would go directly to the Breast Cancer Research Foundation. The Melee community had raised a whopping $94,683, compared to the overall donation funds of over $225,000. Melee held a close race against the runner-up, *Skullgirls*, an indie game with a more traditional but tag team-based combat, similar to the *Marvel vs. Capcom* series. During the final night of the voting phase, members from both communities constantly donated against each other in attempts to top each other and gain that coveted slot, but Skullgirls fell a bit short with a still-impressive $78,760. Other games weren't even close, with third place going to *Super Street Fighter 2 Turbo* with a notable $39,567.[2] Few people saw Brawl as a competitive game (raising only $170), so Brawl wasn't and thus was never seen at EVO again. Melee, on the other hand, proved itself to be such a success that year that it continued to appear in the lineup every year since. Not bad at all for a game that's now over fifteen years old.

In 2015, Smash 4 was added to the lineup as the second most popular game at the event. This game brought in 1,926 entrants, with *Ultimate Street Fighter IV* bringing in 2,227 entrants and Melee coming in third

1   https://en.wikipedia.org/wiki/Evolution_Championship_Series

2   https://www.engadget.com/2013/02/01/evo-2013-charity-drive-raises-over-200-000-smash-bros-melee-f/

with 1,869. The Smash community as a whole brought in a collective 3,284 unique entrants, with a 16% overlap of 517 Smash players who entered both games, making Smash the most popular franchise of the year at EVO.[3]

Given EVO's prestige and Smash's rise as a fighting game series, this was *the* tournament to attend for the year. In comparison, the tournament with the second largest number of entrants for Smash 4 in 2015, Apex 2015, had 837 entrants (and 1,037 in Melee), less than half of EVO's numbers. Everyone around the world wanted to compete at EVO, with Smash 4 bringing in people from Japan, Mexico, Canada, South America, Europe, and more. The best part of this series, and with fighting game events in general, is that it was and will always remain open to everyone. There were no qualifications, so anyone could partake in the biggest fighting game event in the world. In contrast with other esports, you generally need to be signed onto an esports team to compete on a national scale.

With this prestige and accessibility, the Hawaii community was coming to Vegas in full force. The dream was alive: flying out-of-state to compete in the greatest competition in the world, rekindling relationships with my old friends and crew back from Hawaii (even if I was away for only three months), strengthening my bond with the San Diego and Southern California community, and meeting people with the greatest range of backgrounds and stories to share. This also happened to be my first trip to Vegas, so I knew I was in for a weekend to remember.

To make the most of this experience, about a month before, I started designing a T-shirt campaign specifically for Donkey Kong players, hopefully finding some players wearing it at the event. I ended up creating a design that meshed Donkey and Diddy Kong with Appa and Momo,

3 https://www.ssbwiki.com/Tournament:EVO_2015

respectively, from the *Avatar: The Last Airbender* series, a Nickelodeon show where people can control the 4 classical elements: fire, water, earth, and air, using Chinese martial arts. Donkey Kong's special moves also happened to use various elements including fire, lightning, wind, and earth. Nobody quite understood why Donkey Kong had those kinds of attacks since they don't exist anywhere in the *Donkey Kong* series, but nonetheless, they made Donkey Kong quite fun to play with. Regardless, because of the resemblance, it was common for Smashers to call Donkey Kong the "Avatar," master of more-or-less about four elements. I had the fortunate opportunity to have all my friends in this community help in spreading the word, including DKwill who given his reputation had an immense network to share with. As a bonus, I did make a few sales out of this; however, I was more excited about seeing who would be wearing it at this 2,000-man event.

Fast forward a month and I made my way to the Bally hotel, where the event was held and also where my friends and I were staying for the weekend. I was greeted by my fellow crew mates for the first time since having left Hawaii. Everyone thought that I had improved tenfold for residing in Southern California, but little did they know how I had been attending few tournaments. We grabbed our badges after waiting in the pickup line for about an hour, played Smash for even more hours in the hotel room while catching up on life and Hawaii Smash, then concluded the night with an amazing dinner out on the strip.

I still couldn't believe the whole weekend was happening. We actually went from playing Smash in a friend's garage to playing in a hotel ballroom in Las Vegas. The power of video games—who would have thought?

* * *

The big day had arrived: Friday, July 17th, 2015. I walked into the ballroom filled with awe—I still couldn't believe such an event existed for video games. Thousands of gaming enthusiasts crowded the halls. Hundreds of consoles for varying systems were laid throughout not just one but two ballrooms. Spectators were cheering for one another left and right, money matches were abundant throughout all the games, and competitors were in complete control, ready to win it all. Lightly golden walls and lights embellished about four acres worth of space, with blue strobe lights emanating from the center of the ceiling to portray EVO's color scheme. Maroon carpets covered the entire floor space. Black and white signs stood on top of over 40 tables per room, labeling them with station numbers. In the back of the ballroom that hosted Smash 4, an enormous projector display of perhaps 200 feet wide covered the wall to showcase the game of the hour, surrounded by two smaller projectors of about 50 feet each for other games to broadcast simultaneously. What we were seeing on these extensive walls was being live-streamed on *Twitch*, the primary platform for live-streaming video games, for the spectators from all around the world to watch in the comfort of their own home.

The tournament started as early as 8 A.M., but not everybody had to show up at that time. Tournaments were divided into multiple phases, where only a select number of people in the first phase would advance to the next. In the first phase, the players are divided into multiple groups called *pools*, in this specific event consisting of 16 entrants per pool but usually ranging from 16 to 32. This essentially creates a subset of the bracket, allowing the tournament to run in parallel to minimize each players' wait time. Out of 16 players per pool, only two would make it to the next round in this tournament; some tournaments allow three or more to advance. Each pool would last about two hours, and each group of pools in this two-hour time block would be considered a *wave*. With the organization of waves, each competitor was assigned a time slot for when they would have to play, so they don't have to wait around for the majority of the names to be called unlike at smaller local events. Those who don't advance to the next phase are considered to have "drowned in pools."

Some of my friends had to play at the early 8 A.M. time slot, while others including myself were to play as late as 4 P.M. Regardless, I was hanging around in the ballroom for almost twelve hours straight, supporting my friends and coaching them as needed, playing friendlies against hundreds of new players, analyzing top-level play, and of course competing while living on water and snacks. I also met some people who recognized me through my shirt, including a few who were wearing it themselves! Everything was perfect: the new friendships, the rejoicing, and of course the competition in doing what we all love.

4 P.M. came along, and I rushed my way from the friendlies area to my pool station to check in. No recognizable names in my pool. I can do this. I was winning most of my friendlies, HiD was hanging around for support, and I was in a fantastic mood thanks to my T-shirt campaign. Time to show the world what I've got.

First round is against a Rosalina and Luma[4], who is actually considered Donkey Kong's worst matchup, if not one of the worst matchup pairings in the entire game. Since each character has unique strengths and weaknesses, many matchups are not evenly matched. One character's strengths can heavily and easily capitalize on another character's weaknesses. I wasn't going to let this stop me, however. After the first few seconds into the match, I could tell that my first opponent

---

4   Rosalina and Luma, making their Smash debut from the *Super Mario* series, are a pair of playable characters known for their strong defensive play. Luma, a support character in the shape of a star, fights in front of Rosalina and mimics her inputs while having its own health bar and indefinite number of respawns after a fixed amount of time after its death. These attributes place them as one of the best characters in the game.

wasn't as experienced, but the character itself made the match much more difficult than expected. I was able to scrape by, winning my first set at a national tournament. Awesome.

Fortunately or unfortunately, the rest of the pool actually seemed to be rather easy and... anti-climatic. My match in the grand finals of my pool was against a Bowser[5] who was also the pool captain, the person announcing matches and recording their scores for this pool. He claimed that he did not play Smash much and joined just because he was here at EVO, prioritizing other games instead. He also admitted that he had no idea how he reached that far in the bracket. Regardless, he still was not a bad player at all, putting up a fight as I almost lost both games, but I managed to make it out of pools without dropping a single game.

The second phase was scheduled to start in the next two-hour time slot at 6 P.M., but the tournament was running late and so my next match ended up starting about 45 minutes in. My first opponent in this round was a fellow Southern California player, a male Wii Fit Trainer[6] player (this character can be played as either gender, but female is the default version). I actually had not fought let alone seen a single Wii Fit Trainer in a tournament before, so I went into that match not knowing what to expect at all (I don't even think I had fought against this character in friendlies at that time), but after playing the match for a good minute it felt like his inexperience against Donkey Kong was similar. This was one of the most intense matches I've had yet. My initial reaction was that he seemed to be the stronger player, yet the match still felt winnable, with all the pressure he was throwing at me yet with blind spots in his

---

5   Bowser, the antagonist from the *Super Mario* series, is considered a mid-tiered character known for his survivability, immense kill power, and intimidating grab range and combos.

6   Wii Fit Trainer, from the *Wii Fit* series, is considered a low-tiered character known for her evasiveness and strong use of projectiles. Her range in her close-up attacks however are limited, and so she has difficulty fighting characters who can get past her projectiles.

barrage of projectiles.

A crowd suddenly surrounded us, intensifying the match that much more with shouting coming from all over. My opponent had a coach behind him who would continuously shout profusely during the match, both encouraging him and belittling Donkey Kong as a low tier character. He would also provide tips in between games, which was allowed here just like at Kawaii Kon. Behind me was my crew providing support, as well as a surprise visit from none other than DKwill who provided advice condensed enough for me to digest right there and then.

The crowd was insane with over a dozen people surrounding a tiny T.V, an experience I was not used to at all. Through my headphones blasting K-pop music, I could barely hear both my friends chanting my tag as well as my opponent's coach with degrading remarks such as "He's just spamming! He's a fraud!" The energy in the area was unmatched, especially given how close the set was. The Wii Fit Trainer ended up winning the set in a last-hit situation on game three.

After taking the loss and commending him on a great game, my friends came up to me excited over everything that just happened. From how they hated the coach to how with one more correct decision I could have won the set, the energy within the immediate vicinity was at an all-time high. DKwill also came up to me mentioning how difficult the match can be for Donkey Kong and how he did not appreciate the coach's demeanor. But hey, if esports can be considered sports, this has to come with the package too, right?

Not too long after, I was up against another fellow Southern California player, this time being one of my first Smash friends from the Los Angeles area. "TLTC," now known as the best Palutena[7] player in the world, was

---

7   Palutena is another newcomer to the Smash series, originating from the *Kid Icarus* universe. She was known to be one of the worst characters in the game due to her slower ground attacks and limited, therefore predictable, playstyle. Her strengths however lie in her

a newer up-and-coming player at that time. Just a few weeks before, I had taught him how to fight against Donkey Kong, and I was actually winning a good number of our matches. Just a good hour or two later, however, he figured out the matchup rather quickly and started to win practically every match we played. Unfortunately, similar results followed in the losers bracket, and I lost my second set in a row, officially getting eliminated from the tournament. Neither of us wanted it to end this way, and thus after the match, we simply hugged it out as I wished him the best of luck through the rest of his run. Friends eliminating each other in a tournament of any scale will always happen, but sometimes that's just how competition goes.

Despite losing all of my matches in phase two, making it out of pools without losing a set had put me in 65th place out of 1,926 players. That put me around the 95th percentile, which actually felt incredible given my first major tournament out-of-state. My fellow Hawaii Smashers placed with similar results, putting us on the map when most of the Smash community was unaware of an existing Smash region training in the middle of the Pacific Ocean.

Next event, however, I planned to do even better. I loved seeing how much more I had to go. I had high hopes for the future, realizing my potential is limitless with my growth mindset, and I was confident in knowing the world would soon know my name as an up-and-coming threat. I learned so much by playing against the plethora of fellow competitors here, both in the tournament and in friendlies. Compared to Hawaii, this was a knowledge gold mine. There's just so much information to take in—the learning never stops. Perhaps that's why fighting games are so fascinating to me, on top of the sheer entertainment of unrealized

---

great mobility and combos following a grab. Despite the community's opinions on her at the time, a Palutena player eventually knocks out the undisputed best player in the world in a later international tournament.

possibilities that could occur in any match. You really never know what to expect. Learning aside, this was basically a grand arcade room with thousands of people to play against, and how can any gamer not have fun with that?

Although my tournament run was over, there was still plenty to enjoy at EVO and the rest of Vegas—after all, it was still only Friday, and technically the weekend hadn't even started yet! My friends and I enjoyed watching other games even though we didn't play them, went out for dinner on the strip again and explored the rest of Vegas, then spent the rest of the evening playing even more friendlies in our hotel rooms. The next day we woke up to watching top 8 in the same ballroom at noon, live for our first time. More friendlies, more food, and we even decided to tune in to the aquatic stage of Cirque du Soleil's *O* at the Bellagio hotel. Sunday consisted of an all-you-can-eat at Bacchanal Buffet in Caesar's Palace before we all had to head back home and return to the reality of our everyday lives. Sunday also consisted of top 8 brackets for other games, but we weren't too interested in tuning in to those matches this time around compared to what the rest of Vegas had to offer, as I wasn't the only one in the group who was experiencing Vegas for the first time.

With so much to do, it was a trip to remember. I couldn't believe that this was simply my first of many national tournaments soon to come. After this past weekend, I wanted to attend so much more! I would meet as many people as possible, explore the nation's or even perhaps the world's different regions and cities, see what other tournaments had to offer, and maybe eventually make a name for myself. Especially having come from Hawaii, traveling anywhere within the states from my original home would cost an arm and a leg, but now after having moved to the contiguous states, there were so many more opportunities available (and for my actual career as well). There was so much more to come, and I couldn't be more excited. Little did I know at that time, thanks to that decision, Smash 4 would make the next three to four years the time of my life.

Chapter Seven

The Solo Traveler Archives

Over the next three years, I gathered up the courage to travel all across the nation—solo. Not all of my trips, but maybe about half of them. Why solo? Simple: often, nobody I knew could come along, whether due to time, money, or interest. I knew I was fortunate to have become a working adult at such an opportune time—when Smash is growing tremendously as an esport—let alone while working as a software engineer with a flexible schedule. Almost all of my Smash friends, the majority still students, generally weren't able to come along except for a select few who would maybe travel once a year while staying on the west coast. Those who did have both the time and money to travel weren't as invested in Smash as I was, or at least weren't so interested in the travel aspect of Smash. I suppose after having moved to California on my own, going anywhere by myself didn't seem as daunting. I also got to meet so many people in Las Vegas simply through playing, and I was away from my group of friends half the time anyway, so I was confident that I could do the same wherever I went. And just like at EVO, majority of Smash tournaments would be open entry so that anybody could participate—you could count the number of invitation-only tournaments on one hand each year. I didn't have to wait to become a professional to enjoy traveling for Smash, and I knew many other players my level would be there as well. I might be traveling solo, but I knew I wouldn't be alone.

Through Smash, I never would have thought that I would get out of my comfort zone and fly out by myself to a brand new region, let alone over a dozen. However, after my experience in Las Vegas, I simply couldn't help it! I loved the feeling of exploring new places, getting a feel for the people and their culture, trying new food, and simply walking around with no real agenda—on top of the love of Smash. After having lived in Hawaii my entire life where travel was difficult and rare, having left the island perhaps about five times or so when I still lived there, I didn't realize just how much freedom I was given thanks to moving to the continental U.S. I had even traveled more throughout 2016 than I did my entire life before then. I was sure to take advantage of all these opportunities available while I could.

This idea gave me enough confidence to book my first solo flight: to New Orleans, Louisiana. The sense of traveling alone stuck to me so well after my first experience of moving to California by myself. I couldn't stop. This isn't the norm to the Smash community at all—given the tiny demographic who can actually travel, almost all of them cringe on the thought of going somewhere without a friend—but whether you are currently a part of this community or not, I hope I can convince you through these adventures why trying out solo travel at least once would be more than worthwhile.

* * *

I decided maybe about two months before the tournament that I had wanted to take this opportunity. Everything during the planning phase felt similar to my planning for Las Vegas, yet so different due to the fact that I'd be on my own. Given that, I made a list of tips to help those who'd like to travel on their own as well, reminding myself that nothing beats solo traveling if you make the most of it.

1. **PRIORITIZE TRAVELING.** Pick a destination—it doesn't have to be far—and set a date. Make saving up for this trip a priority, as you'll put it off indefinitely otherwise. You'll grow so much as a person. It might help for some to treat it as an investment more than a vacation. With your place and time set, you can now save up accordingly. Even if it takes months or years to save up (if the budget requires years of saving, perhaps consider a closer destination closer—maybe one you can drive to), be sure to keep saving. Compare your everyday purchases to this trip and consider if it's worth buying after all when you want to afford this trip. Notable sacrifices including your daily coffee (replaceable with a coffee pot at home, or maybe caffeine pills), eating out (opt to cook at home instead), and buying used products instead of new. It'll be worth it.

2. **ACCOMMODATIONS.** There are fortunately a good number of cheap options for housing, especially for solo travelers where spending $200 a night at a hotel doesn't sound too hot. My preference is usually with the website *Airbnb*, as you can typically find a listing that's perfect for you—the perfect location relative to where you want to explore, the amenities, and the price. Depending on the city, I typically spend $20 to $60 a night. Remember that since you're traveling alone, you don't have to worry about accommodating friends or last-minute cancellations,

so finding one perfect for you will be a lot easier. I also recommend prioritizing booking a listing that's hosted by an Airbnb "superhost," experienced hosts who have hosted a good number of travelers, have a high rating, and are known to be reliable (e.g. not canceling the day before, having prompt communication, etc.). Another website *Couchsurfing* provides free stays (by benevolent hosts who love meeting travelers from all over), but the number of available homes, especially homes accommodating your needs, are often fewer. Outside of those two websites, motels and hostels are usually the best picks when it comes to location, often in downtown itself. Fortunately for the Smash community, the network of Smash players is so surprisingly small that one can typically find another Smasher willing to accommodate for free the weekend of a tournament, sharing usually only two if not three degrees of separation[1]. Even if not, Smash players are surprisingly more open to hosting strangers who also play Smash than you'd imagine.

3. **TRANSPORTATION.** Research your destination's modes of public transportation, and take advantage of it as much as possible. Perhaps you can find a bus route directly from the airport and/or your housing location to downtown, even if it does take longer than catching a cab. In most major cities public transportation provides exactly what you need, but unfortunately, I still see fellow Smash players opting for Uber instead because it's easier with just the tap of a button on their phone, however costing them sometimes as much as $30

---

1   This refers to the number of chains of "friend of a friend," e.g. Person C knowing B, who knows both Person C and A.

more one way. Perhaps there is no direct route to where you need to go, but catching public transportation could cover over half your trip; you could catch an Uber to cover the remaining distance. I typically start off with Google Maps to see what routes of public transportation instantly show, but even then sometimes it can take a bit more research than that, for example looking up the city's website to find the exact pickup spot or the location of the bus station at the airport. I generally spend half an hour to one hour figuring this detail out, but it's so worth it. Taking public transportation also makes me feel more like a local than a tourist, feeling more immersed in the city and loving it even more. I can't help but spend that time simply looking outside the window, admiring everything that makes the city what it is, even if I'm seeing it for a second time. I'm also spending my time there simply thinking about the adventures to come—or if there isn't much to think about, I at least have a book or my Nintendo Switch to rely on. Regardless, since you're traveling solo, you won't have to worry about others complaining about the quality of the long ride.

4. **FOOD AND ATTRACTIONS.** Try to spend as much time as you can researching what tourist attractions and hidden gems you want to hit up. Perhaps you can find promo codes for the museums you want to check out or a discount through a third-party partnership like *Groupon*, or a discount for purchasing ticket packages like *CityPass*. If you're a foodie like me, try to find out what food the city is known for and where its best restaurants are. There's always that one hot restaurant that has an hour-long line, which you may or may

not deem worth the wait. There's also that hole-in-the-wall that only locals know about, which is often the same quality if not better, yet cheaper. Browse through online forums such as *Reddit* and *TripAdvisor*, and check out the destinations' social media including Facebook and Twitter. This will also help you out in scheduling, as you'll know the hours when those locations will be open. You'll also learn which places are close to each other, so you can schedule a specific day to tackle them all. Remember, you're traveling on your own, so indulge in anything and everything you'd like to your heart's (and wallet's) content—and skip everything you don't like.

5. **VACATION DAYS.** If you're working full-time, take advantage of as many vacation days as possible for travel. If you can pick any date to use your leave, try to take a day or two off adjacent to a holiday. Let your employer know as early as possible that you'd like to take those days off. If you're a full-time student, take advantage of your breaks! While I didn't have much money at all as a student, I still regret not taking the time to travel, especially during winter break (I always caught up on projects during spring break, and during the summer I would either be taking summer classes or working at an internship). I especially regret the fact that many of my friends and coworkers ask me of my experience on the outer islands when I can't give them any answers because I haven't visited any of them except one, the Big Island. (Two, Kauai, if you include traveling when I was five years old). Those flights were under an hour and were just above $100 round trip. Even as a student I had the opportunity to try it at least once during my college career.

6. **BOOK IT.** Book everything you can in advance, from the flights to tickets for an exhibition, as soon as possible. Flights will almost always be cheaper when booked earlier, especially one to two months in advance. There's plenty of websites to help find the cheapest prices for flights, but my go-to ones include *Google Flights* and *Skiplagged*. In addition, you will have already covered a good portion of your expenses in advance, so the amount of spending money you'll need while you're actually traveling will be a lot less. Saving that money will become a lot more manageable. Plus, the less you're stressing about the planning, the better! Get it all out of the way so all that's left to do the month before is to wait in excitement.

With the tournament determining my destination, New Orleans was a place I never would have considered visiting. One poor decision of booking a red-eye flight with two layovers later (for cost's sake) and I'm in the city of Mardi Gras, jazz, beignets, Creole cuisine, and more, at 9 in the morning in mid-October 2015, just three months after my trip to Las Vegas. Following my frugality, I caught the bus to downtown New Orleans where everything including the venue was, sleeping throughout the entire hour-plus long ride.

New Orleans was hosting a renowned tournament titled *MLG World Finals*, short for *Major League Gaming*, a professional gaming league focused on competitive video gaming since 2002. This organization is actually one of the biggest factors to Smash's success as a rising esport, adding Melee to its roster of games including *Halo* back in 2004. MLG was *the* esports organization back in the day. This was the company to introduce televised competitive gameplay in the United States with

Halo 2 in 2006. They brought out Melee from the underground world of competitive gaming, where nobody outside the Smash community knew about the competitive scene. They gave the Melee community a feeling of worth, providing top-quality tournaments in venues, prize pots, and sponsorships. That feeling brought the Melee community closer together than ever before, bringing in more people year after year. Thanks to Melee's history, Smash 4 is now what it is today.[2]

Held at the New Orleans Ernest N. Morial Convention Center, the venue had a vast amount of space (perhaps equal in size to both EVO ballrooms) for a multitude of games, including *Call of Duty, Dota 2, SMITE,* and both Melee and Smash 4. At the front entrance of the main hall, vendors were selling a good number of products including plush toys, art posters, gaming equipment, and of course MLG merchandise. Behind the vendors was a VIP lounge where players from all games could relax and enjoy some free drinks. Stations for all the games were placed behind there, followed by a seating area for the enormous main stage, probably equal in size to the stage at EVO.

Despite everything mentioned, this tournament wasn't too grand compared to EVO. Literally only a tenth of the Smash Wii U entrants at EVO was present at MLG Finals, and similar numbers followed with Melee. People could walk around much more freely. Regardless, I spent a great deal of Friday in this three-day event trying to meet and play as many people as I could while I was here since the entire day was open for friendlies (the Smash tournaments started on Saturday, but other tournaments started on Friday). At the end of the day, I concluded that the overall competition was less than the average skill level in Southern California, and also less than the average at EVO. I came to this conclusion even after having played with a lack of sleep, so I was

---

2   https://en.wikipedia.org/wiki/Major_League_Gaming

feeling quite confident in placing well and making a name for myself, as long as I paid back my sleep debt that evening. Not to discredit the scene, however! Their top talent was beyond anything I could do, but their average level wasn't too much for me to handle.

Early Saturday arrived as I headed out at 8 A.M. from my Airbnb hostel three miles away for my 10 A.M. pool. The plan was perfect: wake up at 7 A.M., walk around and get some exercise in, shower and get ready, eat breakfast, warm up with some friendlies, win. I get on the trolley, a five-minute walk from my hostel, which is expected to get to the venue in about fifteen to twenty minutes. Five minutes on board, and the trolley stops working! "Something seems to be wrong with the engine, but don't worry, we'll get it fixed soon." A few minutes pass, half an hour passes, and eventually over an hour passes with the driver not allowing us to leave for safety reasons. A bit past 9 A.M. and the driver finally releases us, apologizing for the delay as he got off to talk to not just one but two other trolley drivers who were stuck behind him.

No worries, that's what Uber's for, I thought. Whipping out the app, I realized that somehow my phone was not getting any signal. Ahhh! At least I knew the route enough from Friday to get there on my own. It was rather linear and involved only one turn, but I had to literally make a run for it if I wanted to get there not only on time but also with enough time to warm up. Throughout the entire run, my phone still wasn't getting any signal even after restarting my phone and cycling through airplane mode, but it was all fine because at least I made it to the venue! I arrived at the pool station at 9:58 A.M. and as I'm taking a breather, the pool captain asks for me and says, "Come on, we need you on stage."

Oh.

There were two pools going on simultaneously in each wave, with about sixteen people in each pool. Out of these thirty-two players, I was not only the first person of the day to play but also the first person to play on stream. What are the odds? Given the scale of the tournament, perhaps also with the circumstances of what just happened that morning, my body was shaking as I waited for my opponent in my chair on stage. I couldn't even input my controller configuration properly. Things weren't looking so great, but I kept reminding myself of all the games I won on Friday, thinking, *I got this.*

My opponent comes on stage. I didn't even know his tag. He was quite young; he couldn't be older than 13. I assumed I was literally a decade older than him. Despite his age, he kept a stern expression the entire time, from his entering the main stage to discussing which stage to play our first game on. That alone told me that I was in for a tough round one, but yet I was not fazed.

One minute later, I lost my first game. Let's just say that the average game takes about three minutes.

His tag was "CaptainZack," and in our set, he represented an accomplished Peach[3]. Similar to the Wii Fit Trainer at EVO, this was another matchup I had no experience in, let alone one at this caliber. I

---

3   Princess Peach from the *Super Mario* series is known to hang around the middle of the tier list, but many people believe she deserves to be higher. Her strengths lie in her ability to float mid-air, giving her plenty of strong and safe aerial options followed by even stronger combos, whereas her weaknesses include her light weight and slower movement. The floating ability makes her a difficult, technical character to use well, and hence the learning curve makes her highly underrepresented.

was learning there and then that Donkey Kong was probably *the* easiest character to land combos on for her, with Peach getting in a solid 50% average, or about a third to half of Donkey Kong's stock, per combo. Those initial hits starting the combo were fairly easy for her to land in this matchup too. I absorbed as much information as I could, letting it all sink in for a good minute or two while taking deep breaths and getting ready for game two.

Game two was much closer, and the commentators were starting to appreciate my level of Donkey Kong play (only realizing a few days later when I watched videos of our match since in the venue you cannot hear the commentators). I was actually a solid hit away from winning the match. Both the excitement from coming that close to beating him and the nerves from likewise being a hit away from losing, unfortunately, got the best of me, as I pulled off an execution error at the worst time, leaving my character vulnerable and costing me the match.

Later in Smash 4's lifespan, it turns out that CaptainZack was consistently among the top three on the Louisiana power rankings. In addition, from the beginning of 2017 and on, he was constantly considered a top 20 player in the entire world, peaking at 7th during the January to June 2017 season of Smash 4 rankings. Despite how talented his Peach was at this tournament, he later dropped her for the best character in the game, Bayonetta, pushing his skills even further.

I left the stage heavily discouraged, especially losing my first round after flying across the southern U.S. But, *it's okay*, I told myself, reminding myself of all the players I faced on Friday. The guy I faced was just an exception, and even his character was an exception. *I am NOT placing last!*

I played through my loser's bracket, and by far everything was much easier. Not only was I finally warmed up, but the players were in loser's bracket that early for a reason too. While I was primed for surprises as big as, well, that entire morning, thankfully no big surprises came along and I rather convincingly handled the majority of my pool, with a few close calls here and there.

I had been playing for nearly two hours, now one match away from making it out of pools into top 32. My opponent this time was none other than CaptainZack again, who was knocked out of the winner's bracket by none other than the best player in the world, ZeRo. Only two players would make it out of pools here, and of course ZeRo was one of them. The last one would either be CaptainZack or me.

Mixed feelings were in my head: I was not too confident, especially since he gave me a pretty harsh beating earlier that morning, but at the same time I was warmed up, learned how to play against Peach, and knew what to expect of him. *I got this.*

...Never mind.

The match was much closer, similar to my game two in winner's bracket, but he still beat me in two more games, scoring a total of 4-0 over me. I was disheartened. That feeling of getting so close yet so far was quite demoralizing, similar to getting second place instead of third. There was nothing good coming out of that mindset, so now I try to remind myself of this tendency so that I can redirect my thoughts when they come, approaching everything with a more positive attitude whenever I can.

Despite learning about this much later, the thoughts at the moment were consuming me, so I left the venue and ate my sorrows away. I ended up with an amazing lunch consisting of alligator and rabbit, only about a ten-minute walk away. We all know that food easily cures the soul, especially in a city that has nothing but soul. Out of all my travel experiences in the states, New Orleans is easily one of my top three cities for food (alongside Boston for its seafood and Los Angeles for its ramen, boba, and Korean BBQ). Immediately after lunch, I headed back to the venue in a cheerful mood, ready to play friendlies and meet people again.

* * *

Back on the friendlies grind, I played against a wide spectrum of skilled players, keeping up with players who placed within the top 32 and helping out others who placed lower than I did. Some of those who even placed higher than I were losing several games against me, eventually walking away frustrated and shaking their heads. Others easily gave me a beating, not wanting to help out despite me directly asking them specific questions such as how to get around a given move. "Just gotta get good" (or, in video gaming terminology, "git gud"), many of them would say. It was as if there were a positive correlation between another player's skill level and the amount of human respect the better player would give. I hated that! If I ever become skilled enough to pass as a professional, I hope to never become that kind of person who looks down on lesser players. After all, even if we're simply playing video games, we're playing video games with real-live humans with feelings and aspirations.

Fortunately, not all of the players who were better than I was were like that. Those who were both skilled and personable were a pleasure to play against, and I easily learned the most from those players as I could actually converse with them in a well-mannered discussion about the game. All while getting to know them as people too.

I also met plenty of people around my own skill level, attaining similar results and sharing the frustration in being one match away from making it to the top 32. These people were great to be with, both in playing against and empathizing with as individuals. We often shared similar mindsets and values; many of them actually turned out to be fellow aspiring software engineers or other science majors as well. Finding people my level I say would be comparable to finding a running partner who goes at a similar pace: not one too slow (I'd get bored of waiting or slowing down for them) or one too fast (they'll get bored and I'd feel pressured to go beyond my limits). The equal skill level puts comparisons aside while at the same time pushing both parties to the next level at a steady pace, run after run or game after game. These people were great and I still chat with them via social media today, sometimes seeing some of them at future out-of-state tournaments.

I played against many others who were clearly under my level as well. I felt like I empathized most to these individuals, actually. Not only did playing them give me confidence when I would have losing streaks to those better than me, but playing against them helped me in relating to them in wanting to improve. Every time I meet a lesser player in skill, I get a burst of gratitude for all the accomplishments I've reached in my journey of Smash thus far and the privileges I have for being at my current level. And it's kind of interesting. The more I level up, the more people I'm surpassing in skill (assuming they're not putting in equal amounts of effort), and hence the more people I empathize with and feel grateful from. I don't think it'll ever be possible to forget the start of my Smash career with all these people I meet along the way. Not too many others are willing to play against those lesser skilled for a significant amount of time, feeling they're not getting any better, but I'm not going to let skill levels determine who I make friends with.

I try to give back to others by giving them as many tips as I can between games if they're okay with it. While I help them reach their goals, I also become a bit of a stronger player myself after each game, since we've all heard of the principle that the best way to learn is to teach. All these reasons are why we have such great teachers, educators, and mentors in every field in all parts of the world. And frankly, it's just as important to know how to beat "bad" options as it is to beat good ones in order to win consistently against any level of skill. Also important to note, great players never expect "bad" options from other great players, so it's important to develop a playstyle that minimizes these risks and overcomes *all* obstacles.

Only starting this tournament did I truly begin to appreciate and apply the rule of treating each individual regards of relative skill with equal respect, especially those lesser skilled, because we can benefit and learn from every human being, if not at least relating with them. I've recognized this earlier throughout my college career, and even in that one tournament in San Diego, but this truly kicked in here in New Orleans as I was seeing a new face every ten minutes for three days straight. I'd dedicate as much of my energy into playing better players as I would against lesser-skilled players because everyone deserves my attention if they're giving me theirs. This brings everyone closer to their goal, one step at a time.

It's paramount for me at my engineering job to take in as much information as I can, understanding the senior developers' mindsets of why for example a given design or algorithm was chosen over another. It's also just as important to work closely with coworkers who are equal in my skill level as we discover new techniques together. Needless to say, it is equally important to help those who don't feel as comfortable in coding, especially since in my case oddly enough not everyone on my web application project has a background in software—they may also still have unique insights sourcing from other backgrounds despite not having as much experience. We can apply this to everywhere in life, from school and finding study buddies to everyday conversations when someone brings up a subject that the other person may or may not be privy of. Practicing this mantra gave me the perfect balance between aspiration and gratitude, and I believe this alone will make people successful in life.

* * *

On Sunday, I stopped by the venue early in the morning to play a few more friendlies, but I opted out of watching the top 32 and more notably the top 8—the final part of the bracket where every single match from here out gets showcased on stage and live-streamed for the world to see. Instead, I gave New Orleans the attention it deserved, discovering everything it had to offer. While the past two days involved a plethora of new faces and all the games of Smash, I took Sunday and Monday to give my curiosity some attention, wanting to explore everywhere while I was here. I indulged in the greatest foods from gumbo to jambalaya to charbroiled oysters, rode trolleys that did not crash for over an hour, discovered and supported fantastic musical talent along the French Quarter, popped into a number of intricate yet beautiful art galleries, walked along the glistening Mississippi River, checked out the history behind Mardi Gras, ventured into the depths of the most beautiful cemeteries, gained a deeper understanding of the underappreciated World War II at its national museum, and so much more. Best of all, I was adventuring all on my own accord, indulging in everything I wanted at my own pace.

Throughout the next three years, plenty of memorable moments had come from traveling on my own. I had the opportunity to check out Times Square and the winter wonderland of Central Park for the first time. I got to admire the White House, the Washington Memorial, the National Mall and its wealth of knowledge, and all that the capital of the nation had to offer during the cherry blossom season. I walked around the numerous giant outdoors sculptures standing tall around downtown Denver. There was so much of the world to discover, and my curiosity was thriving as I indulged in as much as I could.

While traveling with loved ones is almost given to be an amazing experience, the joys of traveling alone are highly underappreciated, whether it be checking out your nearby neighborhood, eating at a local restaurant alone, or even flying out to a different continent. Traveling solo is actually surprisingly easier than many think thanks to modern technology. We have smartphones to access everything we need at any moment, from guidebooks to maps to rideshare calls. We have services like Airbnb that are easy to use to plan our journeys months in advance. We're so fortunate to live in this time period where everything is literally in the power of our hands. Don't let the lack of others stop you from discovering the world that awaits your presence.

This trip proved that even the average person can create an amazing experience through a simple video game, all on their own. It went way beyond playing games alone in a basement. It meant traveling with a purpose—for more than just doing touristy things and crossing off bucket lists (but also having the opportunity to do so). It meant forming meaningful relationships with people from across the world, all who share the same interest but have grown up with different backgrounds. It meant creating stories and sharing memories, building real connections. Even the Smash players who don't travel share the same opportunities of meeting dozens if not hundreds of other people due to the nature of how big it has grown and how many people appreciate this game.

The world is waiting for your arrival. Don't let your friends' schedules stop you. Wherever you end up going, give the world your undivided attention. Whether it be for Smash or any other purpose, you'll be glad you did.

Chapter Eight

ZeRo to Hero

Oftentimes, video games are an amazing form of entertainment, even if you're not the one holding the controller. In fact, spectating video games has evolved so much within the past decade. Gamers can make a living off streaming the games they play as their personalities shine, whether they get furious in failing to beat the boss or they're showing true bliss in finally conquering their goal they've been working at for weeks. Oftentimes, even professional gamers can struggle for hours on a given boss or task; just because they're one of the best at a particular game doesn't mean they're amazing at every game in existence. Spectators can also choose to save money on not buying a game, instead of playing the game vicariously through people streaming. Personally, I opt out of buying games that are considered too easy but are still considered amazing, or I watch games for consoles I don't own. Some individuals even go as far as donating thousands of dollars to their favorite streamer just to ensure the player continues making a living out of what they love. A decade ago, nobody would have ever considered watching strangers play video games enjoyable at all, but with the given technology we now have in addition to how advanced the latest video games have become, you cannot deny now how popular spectating video games have become.

Not only do spectators enjoy watching their favorite gamer play a variety of single-player games, but they also enjoy watching esports: tournament footage of players facing each other as they fight for the gold. Streaming tournaments have become such an integral part of esports as a whole: after all, without viewership, nobody would know about these tournaments. Without support, nobody would care about how well these competitors play. If nobody cared, sponsors and partners wouldn't support their players and tournaments. Making a career out of esports would be impossible.

The question now is, why do people enjoy watching esports? It's not quite the same as watching a streamer where they can interact with the spectators. Even if the streamer doesn't interact with the chat, their personalities shine brighter than ever. For the most part, you're just watching the competition. And people have seen footage of these games already, sometimes for over hundreds of hours. Why do people choose to see the same thing over and over?

The same can actually be said for watching traditional sports. The amount of overlap between these two fields is striking; perhaps that's why the only difference between the two is the letter 'e.' That said, why do tens of thousands pay hundreds to fill up a football stadium? How did the Super Bowl XLV garner over 103,000 attendees when the cheapest ticket is over $3000? Why did over 111 million worldwide viewers choose to spend their day watching this one game[1]? Here's my take on what makes watching both games and sports great:

---

1   https://tvbythenumbers.zap2it.com/featured/super-bowl-xlv-poised-to-break-viewing-records-ties-1987-with-highest-overnight-ratings-ever/81684/

1. **UNDETERMINED OUTCOME.** Our brains are designed for us to be curious creatures. Curiosity has carried our society to what it is today, from inventions and creations to discoveries of the universe. Curiosity is why we love watching a story unfold, discovering a character's successes and failures, and watching how one overcomes their obstacles. The world is made up of stories, from passing down the histories of families and cultures, watching the latest shows and movies, and reading centuries-old classics. In traditional sports, people cheer for their favorite teams, excited in their seats not knowing who will come up on top and unaware of what plays are about to unfold (and hence why games that historically lean toward one side winning garner fewer viewers). Likewise in esports, we love watching how upcoming players rise to the top, how the best players in the world fall, how players overcome bad matchups, how competitors finally conquer their demons, and so much more. Both sports and esports share a story that reveals who will come out on top, and the players are the writers.

2. **YOU CAN DO THAT?!** From shooting a shot halfway across the basketball court to watching a never-before-seen combo in Smash, one thing that separates the professionals from the rest is their exceptional skill that the general populace cannot replicate. Recognizing an opening, followed by flawlessly executing the one combo they've practiced for hours, all while under pressure, is a beautiful scene to behold. In the gaming world where the majority of live spectators are also competing in the same event, people are taking mental notes left and right in how they can implement the same tactics in

their own matches, absorbing as much information as they can so they too can come out on top. No matter how many matches one has watched, there always seems to be something new every single time, even years later (and for Melee, even over nearly two decades later). In every tournament, the professionals are always redefining the world of competitive Smash and how we think about the game.

3. **BELONGING.** Spectating sports is such a fantastic form of socialization. People gather together cheering for their favorites left and right. Friends and even strangers bond over a shared activity, connecting with a larger body of fellow enthusiasts. In everyday conversation, sports are one of the safest topics to bring up, as a good majority of the world is able to talk about at least one sport. In the book *Social: Why Our Brains Are Wired To Connect* by Matthew Lieberman, he argues that connecting with others is biologically the most fundamental task as human beings—even more than food and shelter. He claims that when our brain is inactive, it is actually priming itself for social activity, and greater social activity in the brain has been linked to a multitude of health benefits and longevity, even for people with social and mental disorders. This sense of belonging is just so important. The best part about spectating? Anybody can spectate. Even if they only know the basics of the sport, such as getting basketballs in hoops to score points, simply admiring what the human body is capable of can be exciting in itself. In a video game, just seeing cool action shots left and right never gets old. Smash is no exception. Despite your placement in the tournament, or even if you don't compete, we all love

watching the best play their best, together. Even when I'm watching a tournament match by myself, I can talk about the latest play with a stranger next to me, and that person will almost always return the conversation. This sense of belonging is also a big reason for having fan favorites, whether watching your region succeed or your favorite Smash player using the same character as you. Talking about your favorite team, player, or character with others who share the same interest is so effortless, and people build friendships that last for years, thanks to these similarities. My friendship with DKwill, for example, would not be nearly close to what it is today if it weren't for our shared interest in Donkey Kong.

I'm actually not much of a sports person myself, but when I'm watching Smash, I can sit there and watch for hours on end, just thinking about every little play that happens. I not only appreciate watching sick combos executed flawlessly, but I also love dissecting the little plays and the decision-making behind each action. Maybe the lack of sports enjoyment for me is because of all the commercials, or the plentiful number of interruptions between each play, such as watching a football game for over three hours when there was only about one hour of actual play. Maybe it's because I don't play the sports myself, except maybe a casual ten-minute break shooting hoops at work. And similarly, if you can't find any interest in watching esports, that's okay! I can at least understand why people have a love for watching sports, and I hope others can understand similarly why people love watching esports, even if they don't necessarily enjoy it themselves.

* * *

In the next two chapters, I'd like to share a few stories that make up Smash 4's history. These stories are what keep spectators interested years after the game's release. Competitors lived through these storylines, feeling like they truly belong in a community worth living in. They've felt the palpable energy that unleashes on the grand stage, whether that be of victory or despair. Although Smash 4 had only lasted four years, those short years have been an emotional roller coaster for everyone, both spectators and competitors, not knowing what they were getting into.

Fifty-Six

Let's talk about ZeRo for a moment. Any Smash 4 player can tell you ZeRo's backstory and the impact he's left on Smash history.

Gonzalo "ZeRo" Barrios originally resided in Chile, known as one of the best players in his region, although it didn't mean much to him given it was a small region for Smash. He loved the game so much. He asked his mom if he could give Smash a chance—giving it one year to see if he could make it a full-time career instead of going to school to become a lawyer. He moved to the east coast of the United States in 2012, where most of the action was happening in Brawl. While he became well-known to be one of the top ten Brawl players in the world, he was still barely scraping by financially. He even competed in Melee and *Project M*, a community-based modification of Brawl due to how anti-competitive Brawl was compared to Melee, trying to rake in as much earnings as possible. Compared to his living conditions in Chile, however (he would joke about the days when he used to share dog food with his dog), everything was much better. He was able to survive with a roof above his head doing what he loved, and at that time, "surviving" was more than enough. It was enough to extend that year of giving Smash a chance, now living in the states for over half a decade thanks to esports. He was able to close out his Brawl career at rank #3 in the world.

In June 2014, the summer before Smash 4's release, Nintendo

hosted a Smash 4 Invitational at *E3* or *Electronic Entertainment Expo*, the convention featuring the latest video games for companies to announce and for the world to try out. This invitational featured some of Smash's best players, both from Melee and Brawl. ZeRo made his way up to grand finals against Hungrybox, at that time #5 in the Melee rankings but currently as of 2018 the best Melee player in the world. ZeRo secured the win against Hungrybox's Kirby using Zero Suit Samus from the *Metroid* series, despite not using her in Brawl, or even during Smash 4 when the game came out. ZeRo claimed that if he hadn't won that invitational, despite that tournament not having a cash prize, he would not have had the success he has today.

Later in November 2014, Smash 4 released to the public. This is where ZeRo's story really began. He decided to co-main two characters: Sheik and Diddy Kong, for their safe, consistent character design that would lead to ZeRo's infamous winning streak. After ZeRo's first tournament post-release (on release weekend he placed third at another invitational), ZeRo hadn't dropped a single tournament for months, whether it be a weekly tournament or a major of hundreds of entrants. He had an understanding of Smash 4 that nobody else had. Before the first Smash 4 major, ZeRo only had dropped one set to a notable Luigi player "Mr. ConCon" at a weekly tournament; however, ZeRo was able to win the runback set and take that tournament. Since then, ZeRo hadn't dropped a set in months. In February 2015 he claimed the trophy of the first major, *Apex 2015* in New Jersey, outplacing over 800 entrants.

Between Apex 2015 and the next international tournament in June, ZeRo had won a total of 22 tournaments, including 5 regional-sized tournaments across the country and an invitational in Japan where ZeRo got to meet the creator of the Smash series, Masahiro Sakurai. By this point in time, ZeRo was undeniably the best Smash 4 player in the world. With that, the next international tournament, *CEO 2015*, short for "Community Effort Orlando" in Florida, had announced a $500 bounty to whoever could take a set off him in bracket. Out of 512 entrants, nobody could conquer this feat and the bounty remained unclaimed. It looked like it was going to be a while before ZeRo would drop a set, let alone two in the same tournament.

Three weeks later and we're back in Las Vegas at EVO 2015, the second largest Smash 4 tournament of all time at 1,926 entrants. Despite this size, ZeRo absolutely dominated the competition. In each best-of-three match, ZeRo could afford to lose one game without consequence, but he had run the entire bracket without dropping a single game, even in grand finals. It was literally the perfect run. Nobody has been able to replicate this feat in Smash 4.

The story was to continue for months: who could stop ZeRo's run? Nobody could answer that question until late September at *PAX Prime 2015*, a video game convention in Seattle, Washington, where Sheik player "Vinnie" from New York would take a set off ZeRo's Sheik and Diddy Kong in a best-of-five match winning 3–2 in grand finals. However, ZeRo was able to make the comeback in the grand finals reset, winning the tournament with Diddy Kong alone in a 3-1 fashion.

One week later in October and we're now in the Midwest of the United States, at *The Big House 5*, a major in Detroit, Michigan, with 512 entrants. ZeRo dropped an early set to Brawl veteran "Seagull Joe," a notable Sonic player from Maryland. This would mark ZeRo's third tournament set loss ever, and given the scale of the tournament and how early in the bracket he lost, everyone thought this was going to be the end of ZeRo's streak. After all, he had to go through a monstrous loser's bracket of *ten* notable players. ZeRo remained focused, tackling the task at hand and stopping all of those players' tournament runs (sympathies to the player who placed 33rd after falling to ZeRo in the loser's bracket). Two of those players brought ZeRo to game 5 (in best-of-five matches), but as the saying goes, "close but no cigar." ZeRo survived the gauntlet that was one of the toughest loser's runs in Smash 4 history.

Two weeks later, we arrive in MLG Finals in New Orleans, Louisiana—back to where we were the last chapter. This man destroyed the man who double-eliminated me, along with everyone else in his path all the way to grand finals on the winner's side. ZeRo looked like he was "back in his prime." After all, if anyone makes it to grand finals winner's side, their opponent would have to win two sets back-to-back to take the tournament. ZeRo had only lost three sets in his entire Smash 4 career, so how could anyone defeat in twice let alone in a row? By this point in the tournament, the story was getting pretty old. Let's pack it up, folks; we all know how this story ends.

Except we didn't.

MLG Finals turned out to be where ZeRo's winning streak would finally end. "Nairo," a Zero Suit Samus player from New Jersey, and the number 1 Brawl player in the world would finally prove to the world that day that he was one of the top 5 Smash 4 players in the world. At The Big House, he came close; taking ZeRo to game 5 in one set of grand finals, but it was not quite enough. History repeated itself in New Orleans as Nairo took ZeRo to game 5 of grand finals once more, but this time Nairo closed it out, and rather convincingly on top of that. With this set win, the crowd erupted. It was a relatively small crowd, no more than a hundred spectators on a Sunday night, but with everything happening and with the venue shaking; you would not believe it was only a hundred.

The casters commentating that match would not be any livelier. Nairo was on fire, and the casters were feeding off Nairo's aggressive play. "ZeRo, what are you DOING down there?!" as Nairo punished ZeRo for attempting to recover to the stage from below. ZeRo managed to win one game in the second set, but otherwise, Nairo's winning games were becoming more dominating than ever. In the final game of the tournament, Nairo closed it without dropping a stock on Zero Suit Samus's least favorable stage, Final Destination. "IT IS OVER! IT IS OVER! HE FINALLY DID IT!" the online spectators could hear the commentators shout for their lives. The chat was exploding—you couldn't read a single message with a new wall of text every millisecond. The venue itself was shaking more than ever. The stage printed out in bold white letters "MATCH WINNER" as Nairo hopped out of his seat, jumping in victory and ZeRo, being a fantastic sport, got out of his seat to give Nairo a hug for closing out the beginning of Smash 4 history. Nairo was given a tall, shiny silver trophy, and he held it up high in his hands, never having been prouder in his life.

This marked the end of ZeRo's tournament streak. ZeRo's *fifty-six* tournament streak. Eleven months. You rarely see dominance of this scale in any competition. With such a remarkable winning streak, ZeRo was even praised in the *Guinness World Records 2017: Gamer's Edition*.

But even then, this wasn't the end for ZeRo. While he never held such a large win streak ever again, dropping not only sets but also tournaments occasionally, he would still leave his mark as the best Smash 4 player in the world for the entirety of the game's lifespan while he competed.[2]

Here are some statistics for you. ZeRo had competed in 136 Smash 4 tournaments (of varying scales). Number of times his placing was in double digits? 3. Number of tournaments he didn't win? 30. (Indeed that's over a 100 tournaments he *did* win. Majority of the top ten players

---

2   In the beginning of 2018, ZeRo announced that he was retiring from competing in Smash 4. Although there was a new player ranked #1 in 2018, everybody would still consider ZeRo as the best in the world, as nobody else held that title for three years.

in the world can't even claim winning more than five major tournaments.) Number of times he placed second? 12. Even if he didn't win every single tournament, he was undeniably at a level above everyone else. His dominance would still lead to fascinating stories, as you'll see in these upcoming tales, with the entire Smash 4 community seeking to dethrone the king[3].

GENESIS

Zoom forward, three months to January 2016, and we're now in the heart of Silicon Valley: San Jose, California. The grassroots nature of Smash is no stranger to the idea of startups, technology, and innovation. With the rise of esports and *Twitch*'s streaming services, the name of this upcoming major was perfect for the occasion: *GENESIS*.

GENESIS started off as an international tournament primarily for Melee back in July 2009 but also including Brawl, exclusively to Smash games, unlike the EVO series. This particular tournament, held in Antioch, California, was renowned in Smash history for the beginning of a new rivalry between the best Melee player in the United States at that time, Joseph "Mango" (or "Mang0") Marquez, and the best player in Europe at that time (and still as of writing), Adam "Armada" Lindgren, who made his debut in the states at this event. Mango claimed the prize in a 290-man bracket, the largest tournament by far at that point in time, beating Armada in two grueling consecutive sets in grand finals after falling to him in winner's finals.

GENESIS 2 returned two years later in July 2011, bringing back the rivalry between Mango and Armada. This time around, although there were fewer entrants in both the Melee and Brawl tournaments, this event still had much more to offer: tournaments for Smash 64 and Project M,

---

3   https://www.ssbwiki.com/Smasher:ZeRo

as well as crew battles featuring the east coast versus the west coast. Two sponsors SABERGAMING and Red Bull offered prize pot bonuses for each tournament as well—a rare sight to behold at this time of esports, especially for Smash. The two prior grand finalists faced off once again in the same spot in bracket, where Armada got his revenge for first place.

Half a decade later and here we are. *GENESIS 3* returned from a hiatus, bigger than ever in a prodigious three-day event. This event featured the historic Melee, the newest Smash 4, and the original Smash 64, but no longer hosting Brawl. Melee reached a fantastic peak of 1,828 players, the second biggest tournament at its time only falling short to EVO 2015 at 1,869. Smash 4 also reached impressive numbers with 1,096 entrants, the second biggest tournament at its time as well compared to EVO 2015's 1,926 entrants[4] (Smash 4's numbers in comparison to Melee's made since given the event has a Melee-centric background). Even Smash 64 had great numbers: 238 entrants, meaning that many still played with Nintendo 64 consoles and controllers even after seventeen years.

A new rivalry was finally about to reveal itself in this event: ZeRo, the undisputed master of Smash 4, versus Ryuto "Ranai" Hayashi, at the time the top player in the powerhouse that is Japan, wielding the most fearsome Villager[5] in the world. Despite ZeRo's résumé of a 56-tournament win streak, nobody truly knew who would win the

---

4   These numbers also show how prestigious of an event EVO is. While GENESIS is a series primarily focused on Smash, EVO isn't, and the latter's numbers were far greater.

5   Villager from the *Animal Crossing* universe, also not canonically a fighter, is one of the strongest user of projectiles in Smash 4. He attacks opponents from a distance with a slingshot and a clay figurine from the Animal Crossing universe called a Lloid which slowly launches forward like a rocket. He can also grow trees which can limit the opponent's presence on stage, and he also has a plethora of options for both recovering back on stage and stopping others from getting back on stage. His weaknesses lie in his slow movement and lack of reliable kill setups, as well as being completely vulnerable when recovering.

tournament. Many other top players from Japan were flying down to the states for Smash 4 for the first time—about a dozen total, compared to about four at EVO 2015—and never did so many high-level U.S players come out to play as well. Everyone couldn't wait to watch and discover the stories that were to unfold.

* * *

The venue, the San Jose Convention Center[6], was even bigger than the space we had in Las Vegas, as the event was tailored toward Smash and no other fighting games. Out of three floors, the first floor provided a hall dedicated to playing friendlies. There were approximately 60 setups combined for all games; maybe 20 or so were for Smash 4. On the second floor, latecomers and spectators could still pick up their badges at any time throughout the weekend.

The third floor was where the real action took place. So much was happening in a giant ballroom including singles, doubles, crew battles, streams on the main stage, vendors, and even an artist alley. The hall itself was beautiful. The walls were made up of vibrant blue, brown, and white colors. White lights and ceilings brightened up the entire room. Everything else consisted of varying shades of gray, including the striped carpet, the marble-patterned tables, the cushioned chairs, CRTs for Melee and HDMI monitors for Smash 4, and black and white signs on the tables indicating station numbers just like at EVO. There were approximately a hundred setups scattered throughout the hall. The contrasting red and black GENESIS logo would stand out

---

6   Fun note: *Further Confusion*, or *FurCon*, was held at the same place and time, only in different halls. This was a convention for the *furry fandom*, a group of people interested in fictional, anthropomorphic animals such as Bugs Bunny or Mickey Mouse for its storytelling and creativity. Many own and wear fur suits to show their appreciation of this fandom. As you walked along the halls in the convention center you either saw someone with a GameCube controller or a walking wolf suit.

strong on the main stage, on everyone's attendee badge, and on various clothing including shirts and sweaters spread among over a thousand competitors and spectators crowding the walkways. The artist alley was conveniently located at the main entrance of the ballroom; attendees were practically obligated to wander their eyes around the eight to ten vendors before going in.

Crew battles were *the* biggest Smash 4 side event at the venue. Remember the HiD vs GSM crew battle? The crew battles here were similar, but this event consisted of a bracket featuring multiple crew battles compared to the sole crew battle in Hawaii. These crews were made up of the best players from regions from across the country, including Southern California, Northern California, Tristate, Texas, Florida, Maryland, and Virginia, Midwest, and Southwest. Two foreign countries also participated to prove to the world that the states aren't the only place that's strong in Smash: Mexico, and of course the land of the rising sun, Japan.

This was the first event for Smash 4 to declare rankings for each region. Given that this game was only about a year old, nobody knew who would come out on top. Japan and Mexico were known to be dominant regions, but the United States also had its top competitors throughout the country. And even within the United States, nobody really knew how each state compared to each other barring Southern California and Tristate being considered the best at the time.

This crew battle event would run like a single-elimination tournament bracket, but instead of one player versus another, it was one crew against another. Each crew battle would last for about 45 minutes. With a total of ten competing regions, this was essentially an all-day event presented alongside the main stage for singles matches. There was always an audience cheering, whether it was for their region, their favorite player, or their favorite character. With this pair and with spectators cheering on their friends in off-stream matches, the venue was constantly roaring with ebullience.

Many crews fell, with a majority of them being one-sided. The two final crews that would remain: Japan versus SoCal. With ZeRo on Team SoCal, destiny was revealing itself for the battle to come.

Ranai left a mark that nobody could ever imagine. Japan sent him in against one of SoCal's players who had one stock remaining. Ranai took care of it without a problem, only taking 52%. He cleaned up the next player as well, a Rosalina player, one of the top three characters in the game at that time. He swept *without losing a stock*. His opponent brought him up to nearly 200%, but Ranai avoided every single kill option presented to him. At the end of the game, that 200% meant nothing because it would simply reset back to zero against the next SoCal brethren.

Because of Ranai's supremacy, Japan's healthy six stocks were up against SoCal's remaining three stocks. Those three stocks weren't just any stocks, however; they were ZeRo's three stocks. While we were expecting this match to play in the bracket, we got a sneak preview in this crew battle here. This was seven minutes of intense struggling from both sides. In a bracket match, the timer is normally set six minutes, but due to the nature of crew battles, there was no timer (as timeout strategies weren't considered fair when players begin their matches with unequal stocks). With the lack of timer and the nullifying of timeout strategies, players could take as long as they needed to find an opening. In addition, bracket matches usually use two stocks, but crew battles would use three stocks, so one would expect matches to last about 50% longer. Neither player was used to a match so long. After those grueling seven minutes, ZeRo closed it out with one stock to spare. Things were looking grim for SoCal, as ZeRo still had one more player to go. To America's dismay, Japan's final player "komorokiri," using Cloud from the *Final Fantasy* series, took out ZeRo with 2 stocks to spare.

Yup. Japan is that powerful. We all knew, but after that crew battle, we *all* knew.

* * *

Fast forward to Sunday, eight players remain in the main bracket. And we can all guess who two of them are.

Top eight was held across the street from the convention center at the City National Civic. This allowed over three thousand spectators to sit and watch comfortably at a time. Red and yellow lights shined throughout the hall, lighting up the shadows to make a color theme similar to the design of the event. On the stage sat one table, one console, and not one but two monitors opposing each other, the first time this has ever happened for Smash. The splitting signal to two monitors provided each gamer a direct line of sight as well as comfortable open space surrounding him. Three giant monitors for the audience were hung up on stage: one directly in the center above the competitors, and two floating angled monitors outside the curtains so those sitting along the walls or in the balcony seating could get a clear view. Two casters "Sky Williams," a popular YouTube comedian with a large Smash fan base, and "D1," a renowned commentator with a heavy Melee background, discussed the matches at a desk with a black backdrop repeating the logo, sitting a distance away from the competitors on the main stage. You couldn't hear them live as that would both distract the players and give the players advice mid-match; the commentary was meant solely for the stream and video recordings. Despite this, when you're spectating an event live, you don't really need live commentary. The energy in the hall, both from the players' gameplay and the audience, is all you needed to enjoy the show, just like at a live sports event. This energy is so alive that it's why people choose to pay to see it live instead of watching it for free in the comfort of their own home, just like any sport or entertainment.

Many argue that one of the best matches in Smash history happened this day. Winner's finals. ZeRo versus Ranai. Sheik versus Villager. We got that sneak preview in the crew battle earlier, but those results didn't matter compared to what was about to go down. The match would prove itself to be as exciting as the build-up the months before, as shown in the 160,000 views on YouTube[7]. Even today ZeRo claims that fighting Ranai was one of the hardest matches he had ever tried in his entire life, in any video game.

Game 1: ZeRo took the game convincingly in under three minutes, not dropping a stock. The stream shifted from the game footage to the players, and you can see Ranai's entire body unfazed. Sky emphasized that this game was just learning for Ranai. Minor applause, almost like golf claps. ZeRo was just doing his day job, after all.

Game 2: ZeRo did it again. While it looked like ZeRo would have been able to take the game with another two-stock, Ranai being one hit away from losing the game while ZeRo was still on his first stock, Ranai was able to secure a kill and then some. Ranai was able to survive longer than average, just like in the crew battle, and ZeRo survives having taken 71% on his second stock. The crowd cheered a little louder than the last time, but nothing too audible on stream.

Game 3: The percents went back and forth. No player had a real advantage until the end of the game four minutes later when they both fought offstage and Ranai secured an early kill, with both of them having been around 60% each. Despite the win, Ranai still looked as unfazed as he did at the end of game 1. He knew that he was climbing an uphill

---

7   https://www.youtube.com/watch?v=N9p9ZCoeYXg

battle, needing to secure two more games to win the set. The crowd, however, finally became alive. Ranai was clearly the crowd favorite, despite being the foreign invader. They wanted a new winner, a new storyline.

Game 4: The match was still as even as one could get. ZeRo was racking up more damage, but Ranai remained consistent in his longevity. Percents didn't matter if he avoided every kill move. Ranai in return scored an early kill, nullifying ZeRo's 70% lead. However, ZeRo was able to take Ranai's stock immediately, bringing them back to an even playing field. On the second stock, the back-and-forth battle continued, until Ranai forced ZeRo near the edge of the stage. Ranai kept trapping ZeRo there, Sheik not being able to rack any damage due to his position, and Ranai netted a kill from there. The crowd screamed even louder, with half of them giving a standing ovation. They even started to chant, "Ranai! Ranai!" You could even hear the bias in the commentators, as much as they shouldn't be.

Game 5: This time, ZeRo got a slight lead throughout the game, netting the first kill. Ranai followed suit immediately. ZeRo, however, stepped it up even more, bringing Ranai up to 100% while ZeRo was still at a healthy 20%. ZeRo was playing as safely as possible, only shooting needles to keep Ranai away. Those needles barely do any damage, from 1 to 6 percent, but that's all ZeRo wanted now that he had a significant lead. ZeRo stuck to his strategy, using close-up attacks only when Ranai got into Sheik's fighting range. Every time Ranai survived an attack that looked like it was about to kill, the crowd roared knowing that he still had a chance to win. Ranai, however, was not able to rack up any notable damage, and eventually, ZeRo caught Ranai in the air and delivered the final blow.

Immediately, ZeRo leaped out of his chair, shouting "YES!" repeatedly with fist pumps from both hands. At the end of ZeRo's celebratory moment, Ranai got up from his seat to give ZeRo the most respectable handshake. The crowd cheered for ZeRo loud and clear, despite their response from the previous games, knowing that this was a well-deserved win. Not as many people stood up as they did in game 4, and the crowd wasn't nearly as loud as in game 4, but you could still feel the genuine ZeRo support after everything they had just been through.

With everything so far in this chapter, this was only 2016. This was only two tournaments out of over hundreds of Smash 4 major tournaments to come. Many other players were about to step up to the plate. Dozens of players would start to give ZeRo a scare. Rivalries among other players would start to unfold. Players just starting their Smash career this year were instantly rising to the top. Hidden talent from around the world would show up to new events and make a name for themselves. Like the name of this event suggested: this was just the beginning.

Chapter Nine

Ally or Foe?[1]

Let's take our eyes off ZeRo for a second. Here we have ranked #8 in Brawl. Number one player in all of Canada, both in Brawl and Smash 4. His name is Elliot Bastein Carroza-Oyarce, but to the Smash community we all know him as our "Ally."

Throughout 2015, Ally had spectacular results, but they were often overlooked due to ZeRo's dominance. He placed 5th at EVO 2015, 4th at MLG Finals 2015, and 9th at GENESIS 3. He was definitely leaving his mark as a top player in Smash 4. Things started to look even better however in the following May of 2016, but unfortunately not so much for ZeRo.

Everything changed at *Get On My Level 2016*, or *GOML 2016*, in May 2016, a major tournament in Toronto, Canada. This event was held at the city's Queen Elizabeth Building, a smaller-than-average convention center but still with plenty of room for Smash including all Smash titles and 489 entrants in Smash 4. This was ZeRo's first

---

1 Majority of this section was referenced from this amazing documentary portraying the rivalry between Ally and ZeRo. Check it out! https://www.youtube.com/watch?v=i7TWbinVA4k

tournament since February three months ago due to a finger injury, and in addition in March 2016, Nintendo released a patch update to the game which made Sheik notably less powerful. Throughout the year, ZeRo was transitioning to dropping Sheik and going solo with Diddy Kong, which meant notable changes to his consistency as Diddy Kong was considered more so his secondary than his main the previous year. New characters were also being released and developed during this period, most notably Cloud in December 2015, currently known as the second best character in the game. With all of this, general strategies, or in gaming terms the "metagame[2]," were shifting drastically. Everything was looking grim for ZeRo.

At this tournament, there was a new reason for ZeRo's tag. He had fallen 3–0 to his Brawl mentor and top Melee player "Mew2King," or "M2K" for short. ZeRo couldn't figure out Mew2King's Cloud at all, with neither Diddy nor Sheik. The crowd was getting increasingly louder after each game as dreams were slowly becoming reality. Merely 8 minutes later (about half the time of a standard best-of-five set): "Mew2King! Mew2King!" the entire hall chanted. "The return of the king!" the commentators declaimed as Mew2King brought his throne over from Melee to Smash 4. ZeRo may have lost a few sets here and there before, but this was the first set he had lost in Smash 4 without winning a single game.

With this upset, Ally was waiting comfortably in grand finals winner's side, even with ZeRo in the bracket. ZeRo was slowly climbing the loser's bracket all the way up, just like at The Big House 5, meeting Ally at the throne. (Mew2King was eliminated at 5th place, despite such a remarkable win.) Of course, despite such a convincing loss, ZeRo didn't

---

2　　This term is better defined as, per the website Urban Dictionary: "The highest level of strategy in many complex games, metagame refers to any aspect of strategy that involves thinking about what your opponent is thinking you are thinking."

let anything get to him. Now in grand finals, he decided to stick with Diddy Kong. There were plenty of arguments that could convince you that either player could win:

- ZeRo was coming from a hot loser's run, beating *four* top-ten players along the way.
- Ally had only played and lost to ZeRo's Sheik. ZeRo may have thought that Sheik's changes were too much to use against Ally this time around.
- ZeRo had won every single game (not just set) against Ally in the past.
- Ally only had to win at least three games, whereas ZeRo had to win six.
- ZeRo's knowledge of his character and the matchup shouldn't have changed much since Diddy was barely affected by the patch and Mario wasn't touched at all.
- Ally was against a handicapped opponent; ZeRo still had his hiatus and finger injury affecting him.
- It's ZeRo.

Game one: last hit situation, but ZeRo closed it out. In the player camera, he clearly fired himself up with a fist pump.

Game two: ZeRo took out Ally's first stock after only taking 7%. Ally, however, made an amazing comeback, bringing ZeRo to 79% on his second stock, but that was not quite enough.

Game three: ZeRo tried to get back on stage with tricky maneuvering in his recovery, but that plan did not work well at all. Ally sniped an easy kill with Mario's fireball while staying rather healthy at 43% (one touch on Diddy while he's recovering and his stock effectively disappears). You bet the crowd was erupting, especially since Canada's king just won a game against ZeRo in Canada's biggest major, for the first time in Smash 4 history.

Game four: another last hit game, but Ally managed to find a grab and throw Diddy off the screen. "Ally! Ally!" Commentator Max Ketchum from New Jersey promised, "If Ally wins this next game, I will drink a whole bottle of maple syrup."

Game 5: One final last hit situation. They both kept moving back and forth with the same rhythmic timing. At this moment, anything goes. ZeRo dashed in, waiting for Ally's move. Ally, this time, *didn't* move. Instead of moving in the same pattern, he threw out one last hopeful "Forward Smash" attack.

"WHERE IS THE MAPLE SYRUP?"

Dozens of spectators ran up to the stage to cheer Ally. Ally extended his arm toward ZeRo while surrounded to give him a respectful handshake. "Ally! Ally!" His glasses even fell off while everyone was hopping and fist pumping. Ally was absolutely crying rivers, but he tried to keep his composure as he pumped his fist toward the crowd[3]. "Canada! Canada!" the hall echoed, truly like a football stadium.

For the first time ever, the hero defended his hometown from ZeRo's tyranny. Ally didn't even give ZeRo the bracket reset. This was ZeRo's second tournament loss ever, and from that day on, the community truly believed that it might just be time when someone would dethrone the king, for good.

* * *

Fast forward a few weeks later to June 2016 in Illinois. *Smash 'N' Splash 2*, 261 entrants at an indoor water park resort. Yup, young adults playing video games for over a thousand dollars at a *water park*. The ballroom where the tournament was held may have been smaller than the venue for GOML, but nobody could deny the luxury that is having

---

3   "My glasses were destroyed in the process." -Ally.

water slides minutes away from the competition. ZeRo and Ally were about to have a runback grand finals set, but this time with ZeRo claiming the winner's side of the throne.

In this set, ZeRo decided to try out his Sheik in the first game; after all, he did have a set to spare. Once again, this game was drawn out to a last-hit situation, but Ally got one final grab, throwing Sheik off the stage. ZeRo then decided to try out Cloud, experimenting with wild ideas with perhaps the mentality that he didn't mind throwing away this set already, as long as he was downloading Ally's habits. Despite Cloud being a tougher matchup for Mario than Sheik, frankly ZeRo's Cloud did not look too polished at all, and thus Ally won the second game rather convincingly. Game three, ZeRo won even more convincingly than Ally did in the prior game, not taking any hits on his second stock. Game four? Two stocked, but now from *Ally*. This was the first time anybody had taken a set off ZeRo from two different tournaments. This was history in the making.

Set two commenced with ZeRo going full on with Diddy Kong. In game one, hits went so back-and-forth that they wound up once again in a last-hit situation, both at exactly 153% each on their final stock before the final blow. ZeRo got the last hit as he caught Ally landing back onto the stage, winning the game with a fist pump. Game two went even as always, but in fact, this was such an even game that nobody could've predicted the result. Ally got the seemingly final grab that he usually gets to close out games, but this grab was not quite enough. As ZeRo tried to get back to the stage, he started charging Diddy's recovery move: rocket barrels, acting like a jetpack. The longer the player holds the button, the faster and farther Diddy travels. As soon as ZeRo released the charge, Ally sniped Diddy's recovery with Mario's renowned fireball just like at GOML, having predicted both ZeRo's timing as well as the path he would take. The fireball snapped the barrels off Diddy's back as Diddy fell to the depths, but at the same time, the barrels went on their own path for a split second, crashing right into the stage where Ally stood. These barrels do immense damage and knockback when they explode (and they only explode when they travel by themselves and crash into the stage; if Diddy doesn't get hit while riding the barrels, they don't wander off), and the explosion sent Mario off to the sky. Diddy didn't have enough time to try a second attempt at recovery, and Mario was just too high up.

"OH MY GOD, SUDDEN DEATH!" both commentators exclaimed simultaneously. "An UNPRECEDENTED FINISH!"

This might just be the first time this has ever happened in a tournament, of any level. Usually, a character may just be a pixel away from the blast zone before their opponent dies first if explosive exchanges like this ever happen. Not this time. This was such a rare occurrence that the commentators simply sat there, saying "What do we do?", as sudden deaths are not actually played out in competitive play (the game's official version of sudden death sets both players to 300% in one stock with bombs exploding about 20 seconds in; this is considered too heavily reliant on luck to be the deciding factor in tournament play). You could see the entire audience putting their hands up in a shrugging, exclamatory manner. Even ZeRo and Ally were looking around, trying to find a clue. A minute or two later, one of the tournament organizers went up to them explaining the rules: if two players die at the exact same time causing a sudden death, the game is replayed, on the same stage but with 1 stock instead of 2 and in 3 minutes instead of 6. You literally could not have a more even game. This moment truly defined the rivalry that was about to unfold.

In this sudden death rematch, ZeRo obtained a healthy lead, bringing

Ally to over 100% as ZeRo was only sitting around 50%. Ally, however, got another game-deciding grab, but instead of killing with a raw throw, this throw set Diddy in an inescapable position where Mario kept hitting the monkey over and over until ZeRo was given a moment to breathe a few seconds later. ZeRo gave Ally a dodge in the air, which Ally predicted and responded by giving ZeRo a spike off the stage. The entire audience stood up with their hands up again, but this time in a cheering manner, all with their mouths agape as they were about to see a potential ZeRo downfall *again*.

While ZeRo claimed the third game, that was all he could do. In the fourth and final game, Ally threw ZeRo into the ground, putting Diddy in a position perfect for Mario to follow up with one final aerial attack that would close out the tournament. "Ally, for the second time in history, for the second time this year, will take a tournament from the best in the world!"

Ally's race to the top would continue to rise throughout the year. He took home the trophy for *EVO 2016*, defeating the opponent that defeated ZeRo, the premiere Mega Man from Japan known at that time as "Kamemushi" but now known as "Kameme." Ally continued his reign by stopping ZeRo at *Super Smash Con 2016*, handing ZeRo his lowest placement yet at 13th place. Ally even stopped ZeRo at *GENESIS 4* where they placed 2nd and 3rd respectively. Other players that were considered top 30 or 50 players but not top 10 were claiming ZeRo's soul as well. Things weren't looking too bright for ZeRo, but everything was looking amazing for Ally.

The Curse!

Before Fall 2015, Smash 4 in Southern California was rather unorganized and unknown, even with ZeRo and other major threats (as proven later in the GENESIS crew battle) residing here. A few benevolent souls, however, wanted to change that for the better. Two Smash players "Champ" and "Jmex" together founded one of the most successful nonprofit Smash 4 organizations in the world: "2GGaming," or "2GG" for short. After its inception, 2GG started organizing multiple weekly streamed tournaments that would garner thousands of viewers, hosting monthly major tournaments that brought in over 500 entrants, and funding players from around the world to attend said tournaments. With everyone's help, Champ brought together a region of over 9,000 Smashers[4] and founded one of the highest-quality event series in the world.

These monthly tournaments weren't just ordinary tournaments, however. 2GG wanted something different—something special. These tournaments would showcase various themes, dedicating players and franchises that highlight the beauty of Smash 4. It seemed like such an obvious idea, but no majors had ever implemented this—not even Melee tournaments. This monthly series was dubbed *2GGT*, a portmanteau on 2GG and *GT*, a reference to the anime series *Dragon Ball GT* (a good majority of Smash players are into anime as well). Each tournament would be labeled as a "Saga," with its nomenclature respective to each special guest or theme, for example matching the anime title "Dragon Ball GT: Black Star Dragon Ball Saga." The 2GGT logo was also inspired by the Dragon Ball GT logo.

Starting December 2015, 2GG flew in the top Captain Falcon (from *F-Zero*) main in the world, "Fatality" from Georgia, initiating the series with *2GGT: Fatality Saga*. This event, held in Gardena in Los Angeles County with 96 entrants, also held a side event featuring a Captain

---

4   The Southern California Smash 4 Facebook group as of August 2018 consists of over 9,700 members.

Falcon round robin that included Fatality, ZeRo and his Captain Falcon, and other local Captain Falcon players. Fatality placed 7th at this event, signaling the start of a new challenge: the "2GG Curse." This curse represented the theory that no player could ever win the event they're featured in—and 2GG ensured that they would fly in the toughest players they could get. This created a new, unique storyline for spectators, especially since these 2GG events started after ZeRo was proven mortal where his winning streak story came to an end.

Every month or two, 2GG continued the 2GGT series featuring an out-of-state guest but flying in multiple top players per event, with side events paying homage to these players. This pool of talent brought recognition to 2GGaming as one of the top Smash organizations out there and also brought attention to Southern California as one of the toughest regions in the world. Month after month, multiple top players would rise to the challenge, only to fall. Some would come as close as they could get, placing second, but many others would fall in the double-digit placings. When 2GG realized that no single player could accomplish this task, they made the curse even easier to break: featuring entire regions. The entire country of Mexico failed. The Tristate region failed. After nine sagas, not a single soul was able to break this curse.

2GG had wanted their tenth and final saga for the year as something grand. A theme that is bound to break the curse. Bringing the celebration to Las Vegas in December 2016, a three-day event instead of one, 2GG was going all out.

$10,000 pot bonus.

2GGT: ZeRo Saga.

This tournament brought in 361 entrants, which was considered fairly low for such an extravagant event (with most 2GGTs having had more entrants), but this tournament was *insanely* difficult. Since this tournament would cost significantly more for SoCal players as they would need to travel for this event, only the most dedicated players dared to put themselves in this gauntlet, myself included. Throughout this year, I would win perhaps three or four matches per 2GGT tournament, but here, I could only manifest one single win. My round 2 loser's opponent was an opponent who could win locals. This tournament was a true slaughter fest.

2GG truly tried to challenge the curse as much as possible. They invited and funded every player who defeated ZeRo in a set ever since the game's release. One of the major side events for the weekend, "ZeRo's Runback," had ZeRo rematching every opponent back-to-back. Twelve out of fifteen eligible contestants participated in this event, but ZeRo would still carry out his reign of terror. You would have never imagined that ZeRo lost to any of these guys. Remember Ally? ZeRo smacked him too. 3–0. No chance. This run was amazing not only because of his skill but also because of his endurance, fighting continuously against top players for an inhumane five hours straight with nothing but water breaks. Curse closed. Curse dismissed. ZeRo did his homework and he figured everyone out. All that was left for him to do was to push the buttons he wanted until the trophy was his. Unfortunately, winning the side event was not considered breaking the curse.

In the main bracket, ZeRo and Ally met once again, this time in winner's quarter-finals. Now that ZeRo had the curse against his back, would he fall to Ally? Or could ZeRo actually conquer both Ally and the curse at the same time? The games went back and forth as always, bringing themselves to a game five. Was the curse about to kick in, or was ZeRo here to prove that the throne shall remain his? In the final five seconds of the set, where both players are at their final last-hit situation of the year in this rivalry, they both walk on the ground with similar timing, both towards and away from the center of the stage at the same time. With the most minute spacing in their movement, sometimes stopping their walking for a fraction of a second, they both met up right next to each other. They both knew that that moment was going to decide the match. ZeRo went for the grab.

Forward Smash. Mario pulled back just enough to avoid the grab, then using the flames on his gloves shot Diddy so far away from the stage that the game practically deleted the character. On Diddy Kong's hidden tombstone wrote: "THE CURSE!"

The entire audience stood up. Majority of them cheering, "Ally!" Some of them completely frozen in disbelief, possibly believing that the curse is real after all. In the YouTube recording of this set, you could hear a random man shouting, "I believe in the 2GG curse!"

In this tournament, there was no opportunity for a runback set. A then-15-year-old boy from Mexico had claimed Ally's soul, immediately after Larry Lurr defeated Ally in the winner's bracket. With Ally no longer in the bracket, could ZeRo still defeat the curse?

This kid was no ordinary kid, however. He was easily the best player in Mexico. He wielded the legendary sword user Marth from the *Fire Emblem* series. His name was Leonardo "MkLeo" Perez, or "Leo" for short, and he was flown out to this tourney to keep the curse going. This was his second major tournament in the states, and third outside of Mexico. His first appearance outside of Mexico was actually at GOML 2016, where ZeRo stopped Leo during his tremendous loser's run. Leo placed at a respectable 5th place there, going out in a 3–2 set. At *KTAR XIX*, a regional series in New Jersey in November 2016, Leo and ZeRo met again, this time in winner's finals but once again ZeRo delivered the 3–2. MkLeo would always get so close. Would the curse be just what he needed to stop ZeRo?

The set commenced. Trades went back and forth, with no single side truly dominating. The first game ended in a last-hit situation, but MkLeo caught ZeRo above him and swung his sword for the win. The second game showed more dominance from Leo, finishing the game in a similar situation. Game three was here, and for ZeRo it was now or never. What would be stronger here? The curse, or ZeRo's plot armor?

The first kill of game three was absolute dominance—by Leo. He controlled the pace of that entire stock, bringing ZeRo to the ledge and killing as early as 75% after the hit—and Leo hadn't even taken any damage yet. In the Smash community, we call this a "zero-to-death": when someone claims a stock without taking a hit, but perhaps, in this case, it might be called a "ZeRo to death." During this zero-to-death, you could even hear a man yelling, "HIT HIM, ZERO!" ZeRo, however, does start bringing it back, taking Leo to over 100%. At this point, the crowd started a chant that was often used in Mexican tournaments:

"Two stooooock, two stooooock, oleeeee, ole ole ole!"

This chant meant that either the opponent got beaten so badly that they got "two-stocked," or that a game that was currently running had the potential to become a two-stock and the audience wanted to see it happen—the latter was happening here. Two-stocked meant that the winner would win with two stocks remaining (i.e. in Smash 4, not losing any stocks). With the audience chanting, this had undeniably powered up Leo, as he was avoiding every major hit and racking up damage once again. Eventually, they're both at over 100%, but Leo still had a full stock ahead. Once Leo blocked a hit with his shield, he swung a weak jab that barely sent ZeRo anywhere, confusing ZeRo for a split second. ZeRo threw out a familiar air dodge that his fans did not want to see.

"IS THE CURSE REAL?

"THE CURSE. LIVES. ON."

The entire crowd was in disbelief as Leo's Marth swung his sword high in the sky for the final blow. Everyone's hands were on their heads, including my own and my entire row of friends'. Few people stood up dancing, having made tons of cash off side bets. Not even the best player in the world could prevent the curse from happening, let alone in a 3–0 fashion. Perhaps the curse created a psychological effect that put on more pressure than usual on the featured guest, sure. But the crowd wasn't thinking about that. All they cared about was that the curse was *real*.

Leo's job wasn't done either. He wanted to prove to the crowd that he and Mexico were a true threat to the world, believing that a 3–0 on the best player wasn't enough. Leo's next set was a runback set against the man who put him in the loser's bracket, VoiD, a Sheik main, whom Leo now demolished 3–0 as well. Leo now only had one more opponent: Larry Lurr. Leo had to win two sets from here, but he didn't care. 3-1, then 3–2. The trophy was his. This was Leo's first victory outside of Mexico, with many more to come.

Civil War

"It was your time before. Now it's my time." -Ally.

Inspired by *Captain America: Civil War*, this event, held in March 2017 at the Esports Arena in Santa Ana, California, was formed to settle the rivalry between ZeRo and Ally once and for all. Both sides needed all the help they could get. You had to choose an alliance: are you with Team ZeRo, or are you on Team Ally? This was *2GGC: Civil War*[5].

---

5   Instead of the usual 2GGT which ended with ZeRo Saga, the year 2017 took a different turn with the 2GGC, short for 2GG Championship, which acted similarly to 2GGT but instead in the form of a circuit. This circuit would conclude with a championship round at the end of the year, in which players would qualify for by winning 2GGC tournaments or placing well in them. This series created another storyline for Smash 4, but we'll save that story for another day!

A crew battle between these two teams was about to unfold. It was the biggest crew battle yet: a 10-on-10 battle. 18 of the most popular professionals were interviewed by 2GG's Champ to determine where their loyalties lay. Neither ZeRo nor Ally chose their comrades; their soldiers volunteered to fight for them, and for the $10,000 cash prize. Two hours of intense gaming commenced and persisted as the players dropped back and forth, with each team having to rely on their final player at the end of the day. Throughout the crew battle, the sun was setting in the background to commemorate the wonderful beauty Smash 4 had provided this world.[6]

Aside from those in the crew battles, every competitor entering this tournament had to choose their alliance as well. There was no opting out of this vote. Each competitor would help contribute to multiple determinants that would decide which team would win the war: which team had more members, which team placed better in the tournament (with each individual's placing rewarding the team a predetermined number of points), which team would score more wins in a ladder event (both here at the event and also online for those who couldn't make it), and who would win the crew battle. The ladder events are essentially matchmaking events where the online system sets up two random players to fight, continuously as long as a player wanted to continue. The greater the number of wins a player has, the more difficult opponents they end up facing against (who share similar quantities of wins). In both the online and offline events, a combination of the greatest net wins (after losses) and win-loss ratios were used to determine the highest placing competitors, who would be rewarded gifts regardless of which team they were on.

Throughout the span of half a year, 47 out of the top 50 players

---

6   Catch the video to see who won! https://www.youtube.com/watch?v=NjMqfOxzx6A

in the world were able to gather up the funds to make it to this event, whether it be through crowdfunding or other means. On top of that, Japan's strongest forces were coming in droves, many of them visiting the United States for the first time. Over a dozen of them were funded over a thousand dollars each to compete in the greatest Smash 4 tournament of all time. While everyone respected Japan as a powerhouse region by this point, nobody truly understood the power of these forces. These players were going to skew the brackets so much that nobody would ever be able to predict the results.

This tournament brought in a collective 753 entrants, 2GG's biggest tournament of all time. Everyone who was following the ZeRo versus Ally rivalry wanted to be a part of this storyline. Everyone knew that this would be the greatest moment in Smash 4 history. I myself ended up booking an entire house through Airbnb, even though the event was only an hour away from my home, just so my friends and I could truly enjoy the entire weekend solely playing Smash. The house held about 20 people, all here just to play, enjoy each other's company, and have a good time.

This beauty of an event was one that every attendee wished could happen again. The inside of the venue was covered in red, white, and blue lights, with dozens of consoles to carry on the war. The main stage stood strong in the back of the room to highlight the upset of the hour. Outside the venue, the entire street was blocked from traffic to accommodate extra stages and seating for the competitors. Food trucks were right around the corner, keeping the competitors satisfied while hungry for more Smash; if people didn't want any food from here, the city's main food court was only a five-minute walk away. Drones were panning in and out to capture the glory of the event, and cameras would glide along wires in the sky for steady footage. On this outdoor stage, they showcased a cosplay contest, celebrating the not-so-competitive fans (or competitive players who find time to cosplay!) that still love the game for what it is. In the evening, the stage would become a block party where several EDM artists would DJ the night away. On the last day in the evening, they carried out the crew battle that the crowd had awaited the entire weekend, with beautiful purple lights along a middle walkway between the audience that would symbolize an esports-like Hollywood.[7]

When it comes to the actual bracket, my goodness, it was by far the most top-heavy bracket anyone had ever seen. I didn't even a single tournament set that weekend—indeed even worse than at ZeRo Saga—and I honestly believed that I was playing my best at that time. Nonetheless, I had no excuses for my losses. Civil War did not give the slightest bit of mercy here.

Remember when I said that spectating sports was all about the unexpected? The results of this bracket could not have been less predictable. Upsets were happening left and right. Japan was showing off their immense talent, with three of them placing themselves in top 8, and 11 of them in top 24. Top 8 didn't even include ZeRo nor Ally! ZeRo fell to two players who were not even part of the top 50 rankings, placing his lowest placing in his Smash 4 career at 49th. Ally, on the other hand, dropped to ranks #27 and #45, placing 25th. ZeRo and Ally didn't even get to meet up in the bracket that was themed upon their rivalry. In the end, the master of consistency claimed sovereignty of the war: the best Rosalina player in the world, "Dabuz."

What happened with the crew battle? Team ZeRo emerged victorious, relying on every individual on the team to survive. What

---

7   Check out the beauty that was Civil War here in this two-minute montage: https://www.youtube.com/watch?v=Aae76CdNGjY

about the collective points gathered up by all the players? Team ZeRo ended up drafting more competitors: 479 to Team Ally's 385, including competitors involved only in the online ladder event. Despite Team ZeRo having more allies[8], Team Ally overall still placed higher, scoring the win for that category of points for placings. Team Ally had also scored more victories in both ladder events. Team ZeRo may have won the crew battle, but the true battle that relied on the entire Smash 4 community led Team Ally to win the civil war. While the tournament winner's alliance didn't affect the final decision for who won the war, Dabuz also happened to be on Team Ally.

Despite the final results, the ZeRo versus Ally rivalry didn't quite feel like it concluded there. Despite how amazing the weekend was for everyone, the match between the two still never happened there. Because of that, the rivalry, unfortunately, kind of just... tapered off. They would still meet up in future brackets, but if anything, Civil War seemed to have ironically brought the two closer together more than anything. It felt like they bonded over the shared fact that they both underperformed at that tournament, telling each other, "Yeah we sucked." The "rivalry" still existed throughout the rest of Smash 4, but the energy between the two felt more jovial. ZeRo would start winning sets against Ally as if he had conquered the mental demon in his head, but the sets would still go back and forth. Perhaps the energy had shifted towards other storylines in Smash 4, giving the diversity the game deserved. There were many more storylines and rivalries throughout Smash 4 worth telling, but the ones discussed here truly exemplify Smash 4 at its prime.

Moving Forward: The Ultimate Plan

Despite all these amazing memories, believe it or not, Nintendo

---

8   Pun not intended.

initially did not want to partake in anything competitive.

Let's rewind a few chapters back when we discussed how Melee at EVO 2013 got in through donated funds. Nintendo had announced just three days before the event that they demanded a ban on streaming Smash, in an attempt to keep Smash's reputation as a party game instead of a competitive fighting game. Due to enough protest from the Smash community, the ban was lifted as soon as a few hours later. It was discovered later that according to EVO co-founder Joey "Mr. Wizard" Cuellar in an interview with OneMoreGameTV, a YouTube and Twitch esports news channel, Nintendo had actually attempted to shut down the entire tournament.[9] "They were not only trying to shut down the stream, but they were also trying to shut down the event; the Smash portion of the event," Cueller explained. The EVO event organizers didn't try to object in respect for Nintendo's decision for its own IP. However, Cueller said it must have been the fans who managed to change Nintendo's minds: "It had to have been the bad PR they were getting, in conjunction with the power of the internet and seeing their Smash fans saying 'We want to see this event! Can you please let us see it?'" It is still rather odd imagining a community built around a game produced by a company that refuses to provide any support. It's even more intriguing that the community has to fight against its own creator to enjoy the game at its fullest potential.

Creator of the Smash series Masahiro Sakurai explained this dilemma later in 2018, "The philosophy behind [competitive gaming] doesn't go in line with Nintendo's philosophy in that some of these players are playing for the prize money. It comes to a point where they're playing the game for the money, and I feel that kind of direction doesn't coincide with

---

9   https://www.polygon.com/2013/7/11/4513294/nintendo-were-trying-to-shut-down-evo-not-just-super-smash-bros-melee

Nintendo's view of what games should be."[10] When you hear his and Nintendo's explanation, it's understandable: the majority of Nintendo's audience is on the casual side. Nintendo's games are all family-oriented. Many of Nintendo's games succeed because parents can purchase these games without hesitation, knowing that the games will be safe for their children. Competitive gaming seemed to go against this philosophy, but all we ask for as a competitive community is a possibility for these two philosophies to coexist, with a bit of help with Nintendo's support. While we may want to support the game they made in a different way from the majority, the love we put into this game is truly unparalleled, as many have devoted their lives towards this game, whether through professional gaming, commentating tournaments, or content creation.

A year passed after the attempted stream ban, and at last Nintendo gave the competitive scene a chance. At *E3 2014*, Nintendo hosted an invitational in Los Angeles inviting 16 players to an exhibition tournament commemorating Smash 4's impending release. This was the first time the game was available to the public. There were some jarring parts that made Nintendo look like they still intended a casual audience, including having majority of the rounds free-for-all matches with items on. However, Nintendo did take notice of the competitive scene, making the final round a standard one-on-one match using similar rules to competitive tournaments used today (using competitive Melee's rules of 4 stocks and 8 minutes), on Battlefield, a competitively legal stage. In addition, all of the invited guests had a notable role in the competitive scene from various Smash titles, including Project M. Lastly, in contrast with what happened at EVO 2013, Nintendo themselves streamed this event, on top of the attendance of 3,000 spectators. All in all, it was

10   https://www.washingtonpost.com/sports/nintendos-newest-smash-bros-game-showcases-its-odd-relationship-with-esports/2018/07/05/ad8632fe-7568-11e8-b4b7-308400242c2e_story.html?utm_term=.bede6c59756c

a successfully run event that catered well to both the casual as well as the competitive scenes, perceiving Smash as not just a party game but a title that actually has the potential to go with an esports route, with Nintendo's support. Remember in the previous chapter how we talked about ZeRo winning this event, and without his win there, he wouldn't be where he is today? Nintendo's gift that weekend blessed both ZeRo and the entire Smash 4 community with all the storylines and endeavors we had all gone through for the past four years.[11]

From there, Nintendo started partnering with several Smash tournaments, including EVO 2014, the subsequent year after Nintendo attempted to cancel everything. At the beginning of Smash 4's lifespan post-release, Nintendo had partnered with about two to three events per year, including Apex 2015, EVO 2015, and GENESIS 3. In 2018 however, Nintendo had partnered with almost every national Smash 4 tournament, including that year's *GENESIS 5*, the biggest Smash 4-exclusive event *Frostbite 2018* (even over Civil War), *GOML 2018*, 2GG's premier event of the year *Hyrule Saga*, Illinois's main fighting game event *Combo Breaker 2018*, *EVO 2018*, New England's main event *Shine 2018*, and Florida's main fighting game event *CEO 2018*. This clearly indicated a shift in Nintendo's goals in esports.

From the outside perspective, this only seemed like Nintendo was presenting themselves an opportunity to advertise their upcoming games and products, notably *Splatoon* and the Nintendo Switch before its release. However, according to Nintendo employee JC Rodrigo, the partnership supported these tournaments mostly from the logistical side of things. They provided a significant load of equipment, provided discounts on items the events could not have obtained otherwise and worked with tournament organizers in legal issues to ensure the events would run

11   https://www.ssbwiki.com/Tournament:Super_Smash_Bros._Invitational

successfully.[12] And in 2018, this partnership often included providing demos of the Nintendo Switch iteration, *Super Smash Bros. Ultimate*, or *Ultimate* for short. While this may not compare to other titles in esports and their developers support, such as Capcom's tournament circuit and their contribution of hundreds of thousands of dollars to prize pots, Nintendo's efforts towards the Smash community was looking much brighter than how it was back in EVO 2013.

Undoubtedly, Nintendo had learned a lot about the nature of competitive gaming by partnering with these events. They demonstrated in Ultimate through the design of the game that their primary objective was to cater for this title towards esports. Competitive players noticed a significant balancing attempt among the cast. Everything in the game would move a lot faster than in Smash 4, something that the competitive community loves; after all, the speed in mechanics is one of the major factors in what makes Melee successful today. You could now save a set of rules to run in tournaments, as opposed to prior iterations where you would have to adjust the rules every time you turn on the console. The players' tags would now show during the opening scene of each match, as well as during the battle next to their characters' icons for easier identification for spectators. Navigation through the menus simply made a lot more sense for the competitive scene. Lots of quality-of-life changes like these were undeniably more catered towards the competitive scene, and we couldn't be more thankful. Best of all, these changes should barely affect the casual audience in a negative way, if at all.

"Our future hope with what we've unveiled in Super Smash Bros. Ultimate is we'd love to see Super Smash Bros. Ultimate be the new defining Smash Bros. title across the tournament space," said Reggie

---

12 https://www.reddit.com/r/smashbros/comments/41qiwf/had_a_conversation_with_a_nintendo_employee_at/

Fils-Aime, Nintendo of America President and Chief Operating Officer.[13] With not only Nintendo's support but also from you, the reader, we can make this happen. We can't continue these storylines and rivalries, these young adults putting in all their efforts into what they love, these relationships and communities, and all the wonderful things that make Smash an amazing series without everyone's support. If you ever hear someone talking about spending their free time (or even their profession) in the Smash scene, the fighting game community, or esports in general, your support could not be more appreciated.

---

13   https://www.washingtonpost.com/sports/nintendos-newest-smash-bros-game-showcases-its-odd-relationship-with-esports/2018/07/05/ad8632fe-7568-11e8-b4b7-308400242c2e_story.html?utm_term=.bede6c59756c

Chapter Ten

Win or Learn[1]

"I never lose. I either win or I learn."

This quote comes from a man who was thrown in jail for 27 years for trying to make a difference. Former president of South Africa Nelson Mandela's goal in life was to fight against apartheid in his country. Even after spending his time for nearly three decades in inhumane conditions, he got right out back in the fight for what he believed in. Just four years later, his actions led him to become the first black president. With his political power, he inaugurated change within the government as he sought for peace and social justice, for the better of humankind both in his hometown and around the world. Although he had been in jail for just as long as I've been alive, even that significant of a time period did not stop him. He instead used that time as an opportunity to digest everything that happened and move forward.[2]

---

1   Note: These next two chapters are focused primarily on the mindset of the competitor, so they'll be a lot more theory-heavy than the anecdotal nature of prior chapters. That said, knowing what goes through the mind of a competitor is so important to understanding why this hobby, or career, is so impactful for so many lives in the Smash community.

2   https://www.history.com/topics/africa/nelson-mandela

If Mandela can tackle his goals of social justice despite decades of obstacles holding him back, any one of us can tackle our own goals with the same mindset. Needless to say, yes this does apply to video games too! For those devoted to the path of the Smash career, many learn after hundreds of losses that the only way to overcome plateaus is to move forward with an open, positive growth mindset. Those who refuse to, soon enough, get lost in the dust as those previously lesser skilled bypass them in results.

* * *

There are so many things in life that we want to do, so many things that we want to become great at! School, careers, relationships, and a limitless number of hobbies to aspire towards. For the select few activities that we're obsessively passionate over, we may even want to become the best, or at least try to become *our* best. But what exactly is our "best"? Why are other people's "best" better than others? Why are there so many varying peaks when comparing everyone's best?

For whatever you've been working towards, have you ever felt that after a while, you feel like you've hit a wall? A plateau? To many, that peak is either considered satisfactory (i.e. becoming complacent with your skill level) or a sign of giving up (*I just can't get any better no matter how hard I try*). For the most part, we can't help it since we've all grown up that way. In school, we study for tests or work on projects only until we're confident that we can pass (or ace) them. And oftentimes, even acing an exam doesn't ask for too much effort, at least relative to bigger goals outside the classroom (say a few hours of studying for an exam compared to thousands in perfecting a craft).

If you're climbing a career ladder, working day by day will often suffice as you're exposed to more tasks and roles and you gain seniority throughout your working years. Eventually, you hit a point in your career where it's all just a matter of execution. Even if there is room for improvement, it often doesn't matter as long as we can get the job done and it's "good enough." The latter is even more significant for jobs that we're not aspiring towards a long-term career, especially since better performance may not necessarily mean better pay. Those who want to perform their absolute best and continuously grow in their job mostly do so for personal reasons, but even then those are generally the newer people on the job who have much to explore.

For any hobby you pick up, you might keep at it until your confidence levels tell you that there's no need to improve anymore. That confidence may come either externally (e.g. friends praising you on your work, or maybe winning a contest or competition) or internally (*I can't believe I actually did that*). There isn't much to push you past your plateaus because there is often no indicator saying your best is not good enough. Once you hit that level of confidence, it's often just a matter of maintenance ("use it or lose it!") and enjoying using this skill for pure enjoyment (e.g. drawing for the sake of drawing).

In fighting games, or really any competition where there can be only one winner, that peak will *never* be enough. Even ZeRo who is indisputably the best Smash 4 player in the world doesn't win every game, let alone every tournament. The biggest takeaway I've learned as a competitive player is that no matter how good you think you are, there is always room for improvement. There is always someone better than you. There is always someone working harder than you. Always. Even if you're officially the best in the world, the person you can be will always be better than your current self. Everyone is playing and improving naturally, so as a competitor you'll need to figure out how to improve faster and more effectively than the average rate of growth; otherwise, it's only a matter of time until others catch up. Becoming the best not only means improving faster but also surpassing your plateaus, stepping out of your comfort zone of thinking "I'm good enough," going beyond the defining line between good and great. If you're not ready to accept the fact that there will always be people better, your own frustrations will consume you when you do lose. Learning how to accept losses and to improve from them is one of the most valuable skills in life that everyone should work on.

Doesn't it just feel good whenever you know that you're improving? Studying for an exam, lifting heavier weights, seeing the difference between your past and current work. Exploring new cultures and learning about the world, reading books ranging from business to video games (hmm...), or simply having a meaningful conversation with someone new. When this feeling of growth gets channeled into your passions, it's an inner feeling of euphoria that you can't quite find anywhere else. I think the best thing about this path of growth is that there are always so many surprising new ways to grow. With so many opportunities available in this world, with so many options to choose from, I don't see myself stopping anytime in the near future. I can't help but continue to perfect what I want to be good at (and that's a *lot* of things!). I don't want to stop exploring the world, bettering myself in any and every way possible. Hopefully, with the skills I develop, I can even offer something in return in this world I was raised in.

Remember Why You're Here

Without the intent to improve, natural growth will only take you so far. Given that this is a competition for video games, the default mindset in this community is either to have fun playing or to win. While both are important, neither will help you surpass your plateaus.

Having fun reminds you of the reason of why you play in the first place, and you should never let go of no matter what you do. Sometimes we're simply incapable of solving a given problem (or failing to recognize what those problems are). But don't stress it—we *all* have had that problem before. Outsiders may think that because Smash is a video game, it is literally all "fun and games," but there are just as many challenges in this field as any other. Ask any Smash competitor who's aiming to reach the top—we've all lost sight on what it means to enjoy this game at one point, myself included. I've actually written about a blog post per year throughout Smash 4's lifespan, saved as drafts but never publicly shared, with each draft as long as this chapter. I was just typing my sorrows away feeling as if all my work I put into this game was never enough, feeling too scared to share my vulnerability with the world.

Sometimes our desires are so strong that we fall for this delusional trap: that we cannot have fun if we want to become the best. After all, becoming the best takes hard work, and hard work isn't supposed to be fun right? There's some truth to it, but not quite. While yes, you do need to treat your work as work, and you do need proper discipline to reach your goals, but that doesn't mean you need to toss fun out of the window. It's so easy to fall into that trap. If you're a fellow competitor, remember why people like you are willing to spend hundreds of dollars to compete, to drive and fly out to dozens of national tournaments, to meet new friends and exploring new places while playing video games. Work hard, but at the same time enjoy what you're working towards, and remember why you began this journey in the first place. Your efforts will thank you for it.

Play To Win...?

If you're not aspiring to improve in Smash, that's absolutely fine—after all, this is a video game! But if becoming great is an end goal, playing for the sake of having fun forgets about the intent to improve. We become static in our growth as we enjoy the doses of instant gratification every time we play, just like any non-competitive game or hobby. We just need to be cognizant and have the discipline to focus on the long term, the end goal, as often as we can.

On the opposite end of the spectrum, we have people who compete solely for the sake of winning. Fundamentally, playing for fun and playing to win actually share several parallels in the sense that the result is short-term. Whether you aim to win a match against a rival, win a local tournament, or even win the biggest tournament in the world, winning is always short-term.

Competition is volatile: one miscalculation or one execution error could send someone spiraling downhill both on the screen (getting stuck in a combo or losing your stock) and mentally (losing your confidence and focus). Smash 4 is notoriously known to be more volatile than previous iterations of this series. Standard tournament rules are set so that each player only has two stocks per game, as opposed to three or more in previous iterations (due to the average lifetime of one stock in Smash 4 lasting much longer), so one mistake can be as costly as losing half the game in a split second. In addition, each competitor needs to prepare for nearly sixty different characters—it's often only a matter of time until one fights the character that they are least confident against. (This instability is also why ZeRo's winning streak is so spectacular and noteworthy especially in other fighting game communities.) Because competition is so volatile, I believe that wins and placings in a vacuum honestly do not matter too much. In fact, there are even times when top 50 players end up placing in the triple digits. In the end, *it happens*. But if you put all your marbles into winning, you're bound for trouble when you eventually get the one result you didn't want, especially in this game. Those whose goal is to win are doomed to never reach it at a consistent level and will be disheartened when they realize it.

Even if you were to remove the volatility of competition, the desire to win takes away the creativity for exploration. As the top *Street Fighter* player Daigo Umehara (known as the gamer tag "Daigo" or nickname "The Beast") puts in his book *The Will To Keep Winning*, "Focus only on the outcome and you'll think only conventional thoughts, always searching for a more efficient, safer strategy. You'll wind up justifying your own logic." The problem with "safer" strategies is that safety does not offer much of a reward, similarly to staying in your comfort zone in real life. In fighting games, "safe" strategies are never 100 percent safe simply because the opponent knows what to expect. In addition, these strategies will rarely overwhelm the opponent; after all, they're considered safe for a reason. Let's say, in kickboxing, throwing out quick jabs alone will never net you the victory—they're simply too underwhelming to be the winning factor. These jabs and safe strategies in general when it comes to fighting games are meant to open up your opponent so that the riskier plays have a greater chance of success (and oftentimes, one opening is all you need). Once you let go of the desire to win, the wins will follow.

It's an interesting paradox, isn't it? By definition, playing less safely by definition means taking greater risks and therefore greater chances of failure. But as it turns out, you often need to throw in that risky play to win (even if it's just a small risk, it's often better than zero risks). In real life, this parallels to getting out of your comfort zone. Try out that new restaurant, or that new dish. Go check out that place you've never been before. Take that class you hadn't even heard of. Funny enough, what does all this mean? Taking risks, trying new things, experimenting with what the world has to offer—life encourages stepping out of your comfort zone so you can grow as a human being. Indeed, we've come full circle.

You know what sucks the most about playing to win? Not only does playing to win make us play worse but also the more we depend on results, the more we become emotionally attached to them. By association, this means we're depending on suffering through our losses to keep us motivated to compete. It's only a matter a time for people with the desire of playing to win to sadly give up on their dreams.

I personally have been a victim of this. I decided to take a week off from work in the summer of 2016 to attend a tournament called *Low Tier City 4* with over 300 entrants in Plano, Texas, followed by *CEO 2016* with over 900 entrants in Orlando, Florida since the two tournaments were on back-to-back weekends. While I intended to go to only CEO, I knew quite a number of friends who were going to Low Tier City, including DKwill, a fellow San Diegan Donkey Kong player, and one more talented Donkey Kong player from Puerto Rico whom I met online through DKwill's Twitch stream. While going to two events back-to-back seemed exciting on paper, especially to two cities I hadn't been to before, it actually pressured me even more. In both tournaments, I had beaten only one opponent per event, both who were local players who were new to the game. I was so discouraged; especially at the end of the second tournament realizing history had repeated itself. Maybe it was the pressure of traveling and spending hundreds of dollars just to play video games that pushed my mindset into solely winning. Maybe it was because I lost so badly in Texas that I needed to "make up" for my loss in Florida, only to lose just as badly. Or maybe there was no correlation between the two, and I just happened to have fought two great opponents early, but I was still letting everything get to me. Even exploring these new cities didn't feel enjoyable for a while. I explored with thoughts saying, *Because I traveled and put in the time, practice, and desire to become great, especially after placing better in previous national tournaments, I deserved to win at least a few more rounds*, not realizing the logical fallacy that nobody deserves anything. Fortunately, I had friends to fall back on and enjoy the rest of my time with. I learned in Texas that hot pot after a major is a fantastic experience as we all tossed meats and veggies into a giant tub of boiling soup while sharing our stories and having a good time (even better than Korean barbeque in my opinion, which is the go-to food option for the Smash community after a national tournament, but my Chinese background may have a bias in this). I also learned that for some reason the Smash players I talked don't care for Texan barbeque while in Texas—not even the people visiting here. In Florida, I enjoyed playing the game for what it is in the 24-hour venue, playing against inebriated Nintendo lovers at 3 in the morning using the worst characters in the game whom we had no idea how to play with. Having a Butterbeer and exploring the Wizarding World of Harry Potter the next day was pretty sick as well. Hufflepuff here, by the way.

This lesson of not playing to win had been ingrained in me ever since that week. In the next major tournament I attended, at *EVO 2016*, I placed my typical national placement—one or two matches before making it out of round one pools. Sure it could have been better, but it also could have repeated that one week of horrible performance. Outside of results, I also felt like I beat players of the same level as those I lost to in the back-to-back week. In the next month in Dulles, Virginia, I outperformed myself placing 97th out of 1,272 entrants, my best placement yet at that time, at *Super Smash Con 2016*. Making that placing to me was quite a feat, but at the same time that also meant there were at least 96 others who were more notable players than I was.

It also helped that Super Smash Con was just overall a fun event to hang around at. Even though I traveled to this event by myself, I still enjoyed all the festivities the event provided as well as the hospitality the local players provided in friendlies before my pool. All those combined took away whatever lingering thoughts of playing to win remained and instead just playing my best because no matter what happens Super Smash Con will still be there for me to enjoy. In my losing matches, I genuinely felt outplayed and outskilled, and there was no way I could feel sad about knowing there's more to strive towards. What more could I ask for?[3]

No Ego Allowed

Despite our efforts to improve, there is one notable downside to winning that we should avoid at all costs: inflating our ego. It's the biggest obstacle that prioritizes wins (and we all knows what happens now when we do that), suspends our growth, and distances ourselves from our relationships. It transforms skills into liabilities. It looms right around the corner, relying on undeniable facts that from a meritocratic standpoint we cannot refute against. Despite that, it must be avoided at all cost! The current task at hand: finding that balance between confidence and arrogance.

Having a big ego enforces the thought that you're great and have little need for improvement. After all, if you have something to improve on, you wouldn't be bragging, right? It's imperative to keep that ego in check the further you climb up the ladder, whether in your skills in Smash or in your career. The energy spent on believing that you're hot stuff is energy lost in searching for ways to grow. It's what stops mid-level players from becoming high-level players and what stops top 50 players from becoming top 10. Remember, no matter what you do, there is always

---

3   More on this tournament in Chapter 12!

something to improve on. I've even seen this throughout my career of working in several engineering firms (and of professors while I was in school), hearing engineers say they don't have to listen to anyone, even when trying to work as a team. It's much more common among the older group of engineers due to their greater years of experience. Not surprisingly, they were let go not only because they weren't willing to learn, but also because they wouldn't work well as teammates.

Similarly in Smash, the better you become at the game, the more you'll win, and the more likely you're going to have some egotistical moment. Try to keep that away as much as possible. It will be difficult when you end up being the best player among your group of friends, or when you start winning local tournaments, or even if you have several international wins under your belt. All you can do is try your best and remind yourself that you still have a long way to go, no matter what the immediate results say.

Here's a common scenario that happens at least once at every major tournament: Top player loses in winner's bracket. The opponent may or may not be known to be the better player. The loser goes to Twitter and tweets out: "People are bad at this game. I'm going to destroy everyone." The loser immediately loses the next set he/she plays, often without winning a single game, to someone statistically worse than the winner still in winner's bracket.

It blinds you of thinking logically. You lose composure. You go in with the mindset of needing to prove yourself, of needing to win. It's a downward spiral and can affect anyone.

Here are some other signs that you may need to watch out for, whether you're in a tournament, engaging in conversation, or writing in your diary. Some of these signs are subtle and many probably wouldn't consider it as having overconfidence:

- Declaring you're the best
- Setting unrealistic goals
- Becoming overly emotional when working toward goals
- Feeling in need for control
- Belittling other people
- Feeling dissatisfied when seeing other people succeed
- Redirecting attention to yourself
- Refusing to help others
- Intentionally not asking questions (to anyone including yourself)
- Not reaching out for resources
- Keeping your network static
- Refusing to listen to people who you believe are worse than you
- Refusing to listen to people who have lesser results than you
- Not admitting ignorance
- Being defensive
- Comparing yourself to others
- Craving respect or recognition
- Taking criticism personally
- Laughing when someone does something notable (e.g. when someone wins their first tournament match but you have been doing so for years)
- Believing you can still grow rapidly even with an ego

Being overly competitive seems to make you less of a true competitor in the long run. Another paradox, ain't it? The worst part is that it's so easy to see when others do it, but it's pretty difficult to recognize it within ourselves. Catching your thoughts before they become actions is key to keeping that ego in check. Reread your words before publishing them to the internet. Think before you speak. When you catch your thoughts, try to replace them by asking yourself "How can I react more positively?" This one question will go a long way. Self-awareness is key! The way you react to an event is a choice, as much as people refuse to believe it. Take control of your thoughts and actions, and the results will follow—both in attitude and in your tournament results.

Even if you simply don't care about having an ego (and that is a thing for many people, especially if they still put in the work and net the results they desire), to be blunt, nobody likes an arrogant person. People will remember feeling belittled, and that rapport will be lost, if it was even there in the first place. Don't expect people to help you, or even play games with you, as they'll be blinded by the harsh sunlight you exude in people's faces while the world is busy revolving around you.

People may argue that competition may be frowned upon for bringing out your true colors. Instead, try to see it as an opportunity to better yourself as tournaments will put your ego to the test. If you keep your ego aside, the only "true colors" that competition will bring out is ideally in your skill alone.

You'll also have people who believe that they know all the rules, whether or not it's within their specialty. Even if they own the title that places them on top of the ladder, nobody truly knows everything. It's impossible to know everything, not only because the world is so vast but also simply because of two words: things change. Being a know-it-all never does anyone good, whether in Smash or in the real world; unfortunately, it seems to persist throughout humanity. As the world changes, try your best to stay open to ideas from everyone, even if they are notably lesser skilled than you. Unless it's a clearly logical flaw or incorrect fact, take everything into consideration. It'll often be worth your time.

The Power of Lifelong Learning

Now that we have our ego aside, and now that we're not playing for the primary sake of winning, what does that leave? As an aspiring competitor striving to become the best I can be, all that is left is the purposeful intent of learning. Regardless of whether my opponent is better or worse than I am, whether or not it is a tournament match, I always play to understand, learn, and improve. I play questioning why I lose every stock, how I was put into a disadvantageous position in the first place, and how I lost every exchange. I play with the intent of deciphering my opponent's habits and patterns so that I can take calculated risks with confidence, doing so frequently enough so that it becomes second nature. When I'm not playing a tournament match, I play by experimenting with new combinations of attacks and different approaches, knowing that I have nothing to lose except may five to ten minutes waiting in a rotation, with the potential reward of learning something new and pocketing another option in the back of my mind to use later. The most important thing in Smash is that the more options you surprise your opponent with, the more time they need to process what just happened, gifting you the greater chance of winning. Oftentimes one extra second is all you need to open up your opponent. Literally, every second counts! Having all of these options readily available in a split second is crucial in esports, no matter the game (as long as it's not turn-based like Chess or Pokémon).

Even in local tournaments, still relatively a low-stake situation, I play with improvement being my primary focus. I might go into grand finals of a local tournament trying a new surprise option that I don't normally do, practicing it so that it comes naturally when it counts: when traveling out to national tournaments where I can make a name for myself. Regardless of the event, at the end of each match win or lose I give myself time for a postmortem, asking all the questions I usually do to avoid making the same mistakes in my next match and to improve even further on my strengths. (Not only do I ask, "What did I do wrong?" but I also ask "What did I do *right?*") There is no reason to ever get upset after losing now when you've built the habit of questioning yourself every time, or at least you've built the habit of coming to acceptance if you truly believe there isn't anything to learn from that given match. And honestly, sometimes there really isn't anything to gain. And that's okay. For example, you might just not be playing at a level you're usually playing, e.g. you're having an off day. It happens. Sometimes you make a specific misinput for the first time in years that completely changed the outcome of the match. What can you do? All you can do is to continue putting in those hours, rising not only your performance when you're at your best but also at your worst.

Back to getting upset, I believe anger from losing only happens for one of three reasons: you don't reach your expectations (which you've put aside now that you're playing to learn, not win; alternatively, you choose acceptance), you don't understand how your lost (which you can channel your energy into productivity), or you believe you've overall played better than your opponent despite the results screen (the ego is kicking in, regardless of how you lost). Anger is wasted energy, and now that we have the intent of learning, we know where that energy can be placed towards instead.

Some might even argue a 4th reason: some external factor causes you to lose. Maybe someone bumped into your chair, or even your head, while you were playing. Maybe the power went out in the middle of the match. Maybe the controller stopped working. All of these things, unfortunately, do happen (I've been a victim of all of these, at least once a year for each circumstance), and it's more than understandable for one to be upset at these factors, especially when prizes are at stake. My suggestion would be to try your best to ignore that the match happened. Detach your emotions from the results of that match as much as you can, because, in the end, it wasn't your fault. You might not be able to change the results of the tournament, and sure it sucks to have lost money for entering the tournament just to lose in this way, but there will be plenty more tournaments to come. Similarly to when you're having an off day, acceptance is key here. Accept that it was not your fault—that it was nobody's fault. Accept that these things just happen, as rare as they can be. If it's something that could have been prevented, such as bumping chairs due to a lack of space, it's worth bringing up to the tournament organizer, but outside of that, I would carry about with my day. Your long-term Smash career of constant improvement is barely interrupted from this incident. With that in mind, just keep moving forward.

Choosing not to get angry may come more easily to others, but we can all strive toward an attitude of positivity and productivity with enough effort. To train yourself against these negative thoughts, try to think of each visit to a local tournament as a session at the gym. We don't go to the gym for the first time already fit; we go to the gym for improvement, whether to build our body or to feel healthier, no matter where we're starting from. You may not notice any improvement in strength, stamina, or energy after one day, or not even after a week, but if you go consistently, results will follow. That said, if you're not putting any effort at the gym, perhaps just going through the motions, you won't be getting anywhere. Tournaments are no different. Even if you learn only one small thing from a tournament, it's still one step forward to not only learning but also *internalizing* what works. Internalizing is by far the most underrated part. People will often say "I fell for the same thing again!" but that means that attempting to avoid the same situation will be reinforced, if not just a little bit more. Trying something once and thinking you've learned it for good is not enough; you need to practice the new concept enough so that it becomes second-nature. Remember that knowing is one thing, but application and execution is another; knowing truly is just half the battle. You may also need to practice the new concept in multiple situations. Maybe you're currently comfortable applying this concept only against a specific character, or on a certain stage. On the contrary, if you go into a match trying something out and realizing that the new concept does not work, that's one path you know you can now avoid and will never have to repeat. "I have not failed. I've just found 10,000 ways that won't work" as Thomas Edison has said in thousands of self-help books. Trust your growth and keep marching on.

Once you understand the growth mindset, it's only a matter of time until you will go from good to great to the cream of the crop. You start questioning everything. You start questioning how to question. You come up with deeper questions, and you're able to analyze results and come up with the solutions yourself, or at least you know what resources to reach out to gather more information. Once you learn how to be curious and question everything, and once you learn how to answer those questions, you can take on anything. It's only a matter of time and discipline until the world hears your name.

The best part of having this growth mindset is that once you get the hang of it, you can't help but continue to grow every day. And if growth is the key to happiness, the quest to become the best is fulfillment in itself. As jaded as this quote may also seem to be, "it's the journey, not the destination." It's easily a sustainable lifestyle. It makes every passing day worth living. If you do end up reaching your ultimate[4] goal, that is

---

4   Pun not intended given the title *Super Smash Bros. Ultimate.*

fantastic! However, if you do not, you will still feel satisfied when you acknowledge your daily growth and your lifestyle of becoming better in whatever you choose to do.

On your way to reaching your goals, there are so many benefits to gain along the way as a lifelong learner. Open your mind to criticism and you're bound to earn more in your career, maybe as far as creating your own business. You'll be able to handle more situations with an array of knowledge, making you a stronger leader, coworker, colleague, spouse, and even as an individual, because you deserve your best self. I'll even go as far as to say: becoming a lifelong learner gives your life meaning. It gives your life purpose, wanting to wake up every morning with the desire to get closer to reaching your goals, day by day.

This can be a difficult mindset to grasp, so don't expect the intent of curiosity and improvement to come naturally. I've been loading up on dozens of self-help books over the past few years, and even then I still fall short plenty of times; it'll always be a learning process. We have all grown up with the mindset of performance throughout our entire lives, from day one in school where you need to pass your tests to your career where you simply do what you need to do that's considered enough for your job. When you combine the need for performance with the confidence believing your current skill level is good enough, more likely than not you become stagnant. And as I am a firm believer that growth is truly the key to happiness, I do advise everybody given they have the resources available to them to pursue indeterminate growth in at least *one* thing in their lives, whether it be Smash, another hobby, your career, your relationships (platonic, romantic, familial, you name it), or yourself.

* * *

Competition is such a beautiful thing. It makes competitors at all levels want to surpass their own potential. The accessibility of Smash tournaments (and fighting game tournaments in general), open to anyone and everyone, makes this desire for growth so infectious. Once you get started, showing up becomes so easy. Regardless of the activity, options for the competition are generally available—just not necessarily in a double-elimination tournament. Whether it be a contest where everyone is indirectly against each other performing (such as a marathon) or creating the best of whatever you're making, or you're playing against friends in a wild game of Mario Party, you're bound to find some form of competition.

At the very least, you'll always be competing against the person you were yesterday. Compete against your bad habits. Your ego. Your flaws. Even if you're at an event where you're against multiple people, ultimately what matters most is your competition against yourself. Keep competing against yourself every day and you'll just happen to outperform the rest.

Behind every competitor lies a hard-working individual striving to reach a goal, turning a dream into a reality. Competition keeps the passionate motivated, surpassing any potential they believed they had. Now imagine if these competitors were to take this mindset out of the controller—and to many players, it does. Smash is just a means to an end—a catalyst for lifelong growth. Our values gained from this video game will always be a part of who we are. This desire for growth, for taking risks and invoking curiosity, after all, is how innovation starts and humanity grows! Technology evolves because people take risks in trying to make something better. Who would have thought that after growing up being told of never trusting strangers, we are now one tap away from the cars and homes of strangers with Uber and Airbnb? Art exists because artists are not afraid of showing the world their vulnerability as they put their emotions into their work, from music to theater, from architecture to the fine arts. Businesses form because people take the risk of believing that they have an idea that could revolutionize an industry, if not the world, with the potential to lose everything. Growth is beautiful, and growth never stops in Smash.

Let's not forget the aspect of personal growth, of ourselves as human beings: becoming a player of integrity and character, not just a player that uses a strong character in a fighting game. Players become more willing to work on their flaws, on loving themselves and others, and on becoming or staying humble, even if the reasons for overcoming those flaws are for selfish reasons (e.g. "I want to become a nicer person so I can have more friends"). This makes each interaction they encounter a more pleasant one—and there are hundreds if not thousands of new faces to meet when competing in tournaments. People may criticize that playing games won't help contribute to society, especially if they don't become a professional. But even for the average competitor, if someone becomes a better person and the source of betterment just happens to be through playing video games, that improvement in themselves and their relationships helps us realize that we're just human beings who are all in this together. And I think that's a pretty nice contribution to society.

Chapter Eleven

No Pressure, No Diamonds[1]

"Pressure can burst a pipe, or pressure can create a diamond," said retired basketball player Robert Horry. Whether you choose to fall under pressure or to rise up against the challenge is all up to you. And wherever we are in life, especially in a tournament match, pressure is inevitable. It can hinder one's ability to think straight, asking all of these questions about the match and remaining focused, when you've got something so important to you on the line, whether it's remaining in the tournament, some prize, your reputation, or a combination. Every decision you make—or you don't make—counts, and if you mess up once, if any form of nerves kicks in, that can lead to losing it all. Performing under pressure is so, *so* difficult. It's a significant factor to why so many students underperform on tests, why we can't answer a simple question in a job interview, why athletes fail to make the easiest points, why medical procedures fail, why justice is not served. Societal expectations of us choosing a career path before we're legally allowed

---

1   This quote comes from Thomas Carlyle, considered one of the most valuable social commentators in the Victorian era.

to drink alcohol pressures us into rushed decisions that we may regret years down the road. Executive decisions in business can cost the life of the company. It can be scary because while we have so much to gain if we succeed, we have so much to lose if we don't—or at least it may appear to seem so. There are just so many high-pressure situations in our society, and it doesn't help that they are often considered necessary to move society forward. We can't spend too much time making decisions when others are striving for the same thing, and oftentimes it is a race of who accomplishes the task first. Whether it be seconds apart like in a heated situation in Smash or a long-term plan in business, time is always ticking and you have to consistently put in your all to stay ahead. Learning how to perform under pressure is indispensable, and fortunately Smash players (any and all competitors, really) have the opportunity to grow this skill. Indeed, it is a skill!

Let's face it, pressure never helps performance. Nobody performs better under pressure. In the book *Performing Under Pressure* (how convenient of a title, right?), author Hendrie Weisinger explains the reason why some people believe that they perform better under pressure: they confuse the term pressure with stress. Weisinger refers to stress as when one believes one doesn't have enough resources to meet demands. Pressure, on the other hand, is referred to when one believes that something significant is at stake and that something is dependent on one's performance. The former may motivate someone to gather the resources necessary to meet those demands, and it may even feel good in doing so. The latter, however, is not conducive to anything positive. Pressure is often time-sensitive and doesn't have the solutions that stress has, such as going for a walk or doing yoga. Weisinger emphasizes that it is imperative that one learn to identify these differences, otherwise they will constantly believe to be performing under pressure when they might just be feeling stressed.

In his book, Weisinger emphasizes four character traits that can be easily remembered with one convenient acronym: *COTE*, or *confidence, optimism, tenacity,* and *enthusiasm*. With this acronym, one gains the ability to put on a COTE of armor to handle any situation[2]. I'd like to mix it up a bit, transforming this phrase into one that I can personally relate to and use more: *COPE*, or *confidence, overthinking, positivity,* and *exposure*. If you can learn to COPE with any situation, all the power falls into the palm of your hands.

Confidence

I'm sure we're all tired of hearing this word as if it were the next trending diet, but confidence is such a contributing factor in competition, and maybe not so coincidentally in life. Learning how to build up confidence over time will help you when you need it the most. Keep practicing your skills, whether it be execution in Smash or how you portray yourself in everyday life until they become second nature. Transform your skills into habits so your brain defaults to doing things correctly, or at least how to think and approach problems correctly. Outside of working on these specific skills, constantly remind yourself of the little things to do to build your fundamental confidence levels: exercise, stand and sit up straight, eat well, dress cleanly, think positively, practice gratitude all the little tips we've heard before and are probably sick of hearing by now. Talent shines when confident personalities combine with confident execution; rarely do people perform confidently if they are not confident people.

If the hundreds of online articles about confidence aren't convincing enough for action, hear this story out. At EVO 2017, one of my friends and crewmates, "DanM" a Captain Falcon main, was tearing through his

---

2   https://trainingmag.com/learning-manage-pressure/

pool. He won all of his matches up to the winners finals of his pool where his opponent was undoubtedly on another level. I don't recall DanM taking a stock in any of the games. While he wasn't able to make it out of the pool on the winner's side, he still had a significant chance. He only had to play one more match in this pool via loser's finals. I couldn't tell that his confidence dropped until I saw his first game against the losers finals opponent. DanM was opting for defensive options almost the entire game, running away and putting up his shield often, rarely throwing out any attacks. To be frank, I hadn't seen DanM perform so poorly. This was especially surprising and ineffective as Captain Falcon who relies on speed and aggression to pressure opponents. His opponent was using Zero Suit Samus, a character whose main strategy similarly focuses on aggression, which did not help DanM's confidence at all as he had no time to collect himself. DanM was only able to take out about half a stock by the end of the first game. For the story's sake, I'll refer to the opponent as "X".

After game one, he declared to X a timeout—a break like in basketball, not the timeout when the time literally runs out in a game. In this tournament, at least only during the first two rounds of pools, each player is allowed to declare to their opponent at the beginning of the match if they have a coach. The coach may be called whenever any player announces a timeout, similar to a match of boxing. While each player may announce a timeout at most once per set, both players are allowed to talk to their coaches at the same time regardless of who called the timeout, so a player may potentially talk to their coach twice in one set. Each timeout lasts up to thirty seconds.

I was DanM's coach for that match, and for the entire pool since we figured why not make the most of what was given to us?[3] As I realized his

---

[3]   Coaching in the middle of a set was only allowed during a portion of 2017. The last Smash 4 tournament to allow coaching was at Super Smash Con 2017, three weeks after EVO 2017.

confidence was completely shot, I told him as much about his confidence as I could within just three seconds: "Get down and give me ten." It was quite honestly on a whim, but he did his push-ups without hesitation for the remainder of the break. X must have had the oddest look on his face, but DanM immediately gave me a nod of understanding. For a quick scientific rundown, opening up the chest temporarily improves your posture, helps breathing more fully, and simply gets the blood and adrenaline going. All these benefits scream confidence boosts.

That exercise helped DanM notably in game two, keeping up with X's momentum and often staying even in health. However, it looked like it wasn't quite enough, as on each player's second stock X started dominating again. DanM was a solid hit away from losing not only the game but the entire tournament, while the opponent was only at around 30%. X eventually went off the stage to finish the stock while Captain Falcon was recovering back (this is where Captain Falcon is most vulnerable), but the attempt was unsuccessful. DanM was able to get back on stage while X was trying to get back from the missed attempt, reversing the situation. Immediately, DanM jumped off the stage to deliver an unexpected spike—a slow yet unreactable attack that sent the opponent straight down. It also has a notable amount of time before one can input another attack (i.e. "cooldown") and is often predictable in this given situation, but X wasn't prepared this time around. X was still off the stage, so he had nowhere to land. In an instant, he lost the stock and the game, despite the most comfortable of leads. Only a confident madman would attempt to go for a move so risky, especially since if DanM missed the spike, he easily would have lost everything in the blink of an eye. Knowing DanM, however, in hindsight I'm not surprised. More often than not you'll see wild, confident plays from him that just work.

The roles instantly reversed. Anyone watching could tell that X already lost the entire match, even before game three started. We could all see how rattled X was, despite having a lead throughout the majority of both games. DanM started playing game three much more confidently, moving around the stage like his usual self and taking more calculated risks (whereas the previous spike felt more instinctual, "he's off stage so it's now or never!"). The Zero Suit Samus, on the contrary, was moving around less and using more defensive options, which is less effective for Zero Suit Samus as a character as well. DanM dominated this final game without losing a stock, received a wristband that says "Official Pool Survivor" from the pool captain, and left the venue with the rest of us as we celebrated his and my surviving pools over dinner.

Don't underestimate the power of confidence.

Overthinking

This is a habit I'm always trying to get rid of. I've always been a perfectionist, and overthinking seems to be a complementary trait that comes with it. I've always studied for exams until I could effortlessly score a 100% on every homework problem. In my high school and college days, I used to upload piano covers onto YouTube, but only after recording myself literally over a hundred times because I would often delay pressing a key a split second too late. I fell behind on art projects because I prioritized the minor details over the bigger picture. I'm constantly procrastinating on projects because I'm actively rationalizing my strategy of gathering resources and researching to make the project perfect—this book included. I'm even that programmer at work who leaves comments on coworkers' code reviews saying "Oh, you left an extra space in this line here."

Overthinking at a glance seems like a good idea. You're thinking things through, rationalizing every decision you make, working toward the desire to achieve something great. It means you care which is undeniably an admirable trait. But at the same time, thinking means taking time away from executing. We make less progress because we're too busy thinking. We might even end up thinking about the *idea* of thinking. We get trapped in this recursive thought vortex, digging tens of conditional "what-if" layers deep, stuck to the belief that with enough time we'll eventually find the solution.

Here's an example simplified in the form of rock-paper-scissors. Let's say it's a best of three set, so the first person to reach two points wins. You start off the first round with rock, but the opponent starts off with paper. He wins game one. What is your next action? You have multiple conditional branches from here, any of which you can rationalize as so, for example:

Rock: *He won't expect me to throw out the losing choice twice! The no-mix-up mix-up!*

Scissors: *Since he won with paper, he's likely to choose the winning choice again. That's human nature, right? Like, if I compliment a girl and she smiles, I should do it again, right?*

Paper: *He wouldn't pick scissors since I just played rock. Why would I pick the losing choice twice? With paper, I can either win or tie, but I can't lose!*

As a perfectionist, layer two of your thinking might be, regardless of choice:

But what if he knows that I'm thinking this?

Let's not forget layer three:

But he's probably aware that I'm thinking that he's thinking about my choice.

Etc.

Imagine trying to deliberate through these three layers, minimum, when you only have about two seconds to make your next move. It kills time that you don't have, and it stops your intuition from kicking in. You've trained your intuition to make the best decision after hours of practice, whether it's rock-paper-scissors, Smash, interviews, auditions, you name it. All that's left to do is to trust it.

Simple solution: *just do it.* I'll try to think about the problem for about a quarter of the time I usually spend overthinking, execute the solution, then correct the thought process as necessary after. I get more done that way, and I'm able to learn immediately from my mistakes. In Smash, my poor habit of overthinking nets me way too many losses. My actions end up being a split second too slow and I end up going against my instincts. I choose a different option when the instinctual option is more often than not correct. For some reason, I just choose options that go against everything I learned for the past eight years of competing. I need to give that time investment more credit. Sure, sometimes the instinctual choice is still wrong, but remember that nobody can ever be 100% perfect, especially in a game that on a fundamental level acts like rock-paper-scissors. That mistake can either be used to download information about the opponent to use for later (*oh so he punished my dash in with an attack, so next time I'll dash in half the distance, wait for his attack to miss, and punish accordingly*), to correct your overall fundamental decision-making skills (*I had no reason to choose x when y covers z and more*), or both. Either way: trust yourself. Trust that those years of hard work will pay off. Keep reminding yourself this as you realize you're getting closer to reaching your long-term goals. In Smash, you may be winning more games, getting closer to winning games, or at the least, your analytical skills are becoming stronger. Even if your game results are the same and it still repeatedly says your opponent is the winner, you can smile at the loss knowing that your overthinking is slowly going away and your real-time decision-making skills are improving.

This also applies to everything else in life that demands a pressure moment. Let's use a job interview for an example. Overthinking in an interview will result in the interviewer thinking, *Oh he's bad at communicating, He's not confident in his knowledge and skills*, etc. Let's say the interviewer asks, "Why do you want to work here?" What are your initial thoughts? Maybe, *I can practice the skills I've gained in college at this position*. That could be a decent start to an answer you can go in-depth with. But if you hesitate and instead respond with, *But what does that do with the company?* Let's keep going down the layers like last time. *What if I try to say something that the company would like, but they think it sounds fake? ...What if my skills aren't for this position in the first place?* Trust your instinct and go with your first thought, or at worst give that one thought at most a single validation check, *Is this a good answer? Yes, okay I'll go with it*, or *No, maybe I'll say...* More time thinking leads to more anxiety, less confidence, and trapping yourself into that notorious thought vortex.

Perfectionism seems to wrap up to be a fear of making mistakes. Conquer these fears. Train your brain, little by little. Take advantage of every pressure situation you put yourself in and keep reminding yourself to trust the hours of practice or studying you put in. Remind yourself that one level of validation for your thoughts is enough. It will take time. I try to remind myself this in every tournament set I put myself in, and I've only been able to block myself from these thoughts a majority of the time after about five or six years. But throughout those years, I've noticed myself becoming more comfortable with myself, thinking more quickly in similar situations whether it be inside or outside of this game. If I've prepared enough (studying enough about the job position and company, practicing interview problems, etc.), job interviews become almost natural to me now, despite not having gone through too many throughout my life. I'm able to contribute more in work meetings and collaborate better with colleagues and coworkers. Even in everyday conversation, I'm sometimes able to communicate with strangers as well as I do with family and friends, something I've struggled with for a majority of my life as a shy introvert. Nowadays, friends I've met within the past year or two often tell me they never would have imagined me as being shy, and honestly, to me, I think that's the greatest compliment I could ever receive. That means I'm overcoming my overthinking, my perfectionism, my fear of making mistakes.

Positivity

Keeping a positive mindset can be so difficult, but it does so much for our mentality. It brings out the confidence in us. We take more calculated risks. We give ourselves a chance to prove ourselves ("I can do this!"). It's a fantastic power that's so underrated when society is so focused on competition, doing "whatever it takes" to get to the top. We need to start changing our perspectives from the "no pain, no gain" mentality to enjoying the processes. While the former is great as it suggests pushing ourselves to our limits, it can also imply working *too* hard and putting too many expectations on ourselves. A fine balance between discipline and remembering why we do what we do in the first place is the key.

Despite all this, why is remaining positive so difficult? There are so many factors that are, quite literally, taking away our happiness. Let's go back to Smash for a minute. We encounter players with a stronger resume than ourselves. We end up fighting a character that our character is known to be poor against, or our opponent is chooses a character we simply don't enjoy fighting against. Maybe that player has already defeated us several times in the past. In the real world? Maybe we're about to meet someone in a position higher than our own. Perhaps we're the interviewer when applying for a new job, or if we're already working we're approaching our manager for a favor. We might just try to reach out to our own parents, or we could be trying to ask someone on a date. Maybe we're afraid because the higher power is often the one making the ultimate decision.

Maybe we're naturally more pessimistic because of seeing all the negativity in the media. Maybe our family and friends tend to see the downside of things so we've grown to think similarly. Maybe it's biologically ingrained in us to focus on the negatives because it may be a sign of danger, especially for our ancestors where almost anything could be life-threatening.

Regardless, it's up to us as individuals to focus on the positives for the better. Negative thoughts may be natural and instinctual, but we have the power to counteract the negative thoughts with positivity[4]. It's imperative for us to stop these negative thoughts before it becomes a recursive feedback loop of negativity. For example: *I failed this test... I'm bad at math.... I'm stupid... I can't do anything... Why bother with anything...* It's a task of acknowledging your emotions, then setting them aside to properly assess how to make yourself feel better. This is much easier said than done, but when positivity comes into play, it soars and conquers every obstacle life wants to throw at you.

Negativity loves to throw all kinds of thoughts into our heads. They often end up making zero sense, yet our subconscious does not seem to care about their validity. That silly subconscious mind assumes that everything is true, and everyone knows what happens when you use the word "assume." Perhaps it's biology kicking in again, saying it's better to

---

4   Traumatic experiences and mental illnesses such as depression are another story and may not be applicable here. Please see a professional if this is the case!

be safe than sorry, and hence to think more negative thoughts to be more wary of potential danger. However, society has evolved exponentially faster than humans. Our brains are still more or less the same throughout the entire span of *Homo sapiens*. It's up to us to make a conscious effort and invalidate these thoughts.

Let the negativity kick in. Just a bit. Let it at least show its face so you know what you're up against. Trying to hold back on the negativity is either impossible or draining of energy at an unsustainable level. You can't avoid them; you can only react to them. Failed an interview? Let your mind say, *I can't believe I didn't get the job.* It's only natural.

Once your mind has said what it's said, consciously think back on what your subconscious just said. How true is that statement? How many jobs have you had in the past? If the answer is at least one, that itself contradicts that negative thought, with evidence showing that you have what it takes to get a job. If the answer is actually zero, i.e. you're looking for your first job, then maybe an idea is to give yourself some slack given the lack of experience. More importantly, it only takes one company to take you in. Fight negativity with logic and you'll eventually rationalize the negativity away.

How about in a game of Smash? Let's go back to the story of DanM and X. After X lost game two, his subconscious may have told him, *I lost that game so badly. I'm done for.* He could have countered that thought by consciously thinking, *But I destroyed DanM in game one. And I actually did well in game two minus that spike at the end.* The secret here is that these thoughts hold power because they originate from true facts. We just need the strength to come up with these thoughts ourselves. We need to expose ourselves more to this positive thinking, this problem-solving. Eventually, you'll see the same problems coming up repeatedly throughout life, and you can solve those problems effortlessly.

New problems that you can't solve instantly will be backed up by your fundamental problem-solving skills. Trust the process. Give positive thinking a chance.

What if DanM was not allowed a coach for that set? DanM may have shared the same negative thoughts after losing game one, but unfortunately, he wouldn't have shared the same evidence that X had. DanM did not win a game beforehand, so it's a tougher problem to solve. However, it's still not impossible. Potential thoughts could be: *I played so defensively that game. I know Captain Falcon loses if he doesn't control the pace.* Or maybe, *That was only one game. I've beaten plenty of Zero Suit Samuses before, so I know I can do this.* It's always a mini puzzle game that you have to take the initiative to figure out.

The one story I love sharing about positivity is my set against the #2 player in the world at that time: Ally. Remember him? The creative Mario main that somehow figures out a way against the best player in the world. I ended up having to fight him in my second round of one of the 2GG events: *Greninja Saga*, held in Santa Ana, California, in May 2017. Despite his ranking, I was looking forward to playing him. I loved fighting against Marios. Many Donkey Kong players do, as they consider the matchup to be either even or in Donkey Kong's favor. Every Mario tells me that my Donkey Kong is oddly unique and gives them more trouble than usual. If I lost the set? I lost to the second best player in the world—how could I be mad at that? I had nothing to lose that day, and I couldn't wait for the match to happen.[5]

We sat down at a setup to play our first match. Ally was notably frightened in his playstyle, perhaps because of the threat of Donkey Kong as a character. He knew that one grab from Donkey Kong was not going

---

5   Frankly, I was more afraid of my round before Ally, as I couldn't find any information about him online. He even gave me a run for my money, but I managed to carry through and survive at least one round.

to be a good time, so he spent a good majority of the game hovering around the one platform the stage, "Smashville," provided. All he did was shoot Mario's distinguished fireballs from the platform, hoping that I would give up my patience and put myself in a disadvantageous position. I never gave him the chance, but over the span of two minutes, we kept exchanging single hits. Eventually, he ended up at a percent where I could not kill off a grab, so he went back to the stage and played normally.

Our neutral game even on the ground was extremely patient. The entire game lasted four minutes, even though this matchup usually runs between two to three minutes in my experience. More often than not, whenever we were right next to each other, none of us would throw an attack out, as we were both waiting for the other to make the first move. We both understood each others' minds so well, even in the first game. In the end, I managed to take a stock with Ally taking the game, healthy on his second stock. I remember my thought process at the end of that game: *I took a stock. Sick. I know where I messed up. Let's keep going.*

In the second game, Ally played much more aggressively, as he did not have that one platform to rely on. I took him to the "Town and City," a stage known for its multiple phases, each phase having a unique platform layout. Each phase would last about half a minute. Between each phase, there would be no platforms for about fifteen seconds. It was much harder for Mario to perform the same strategy on this stage, so Ally threw that strategy out of the window. Both characters gained a lot of damage off a single grab, and we were exchanging grabs back and forth. This game was notably quicker than the previous game, running only a minute and a half. Before the final blow, we were at pretty even percentages, but after one final grab, I emerged as the victor for that game. *I just took an entire game off the 2nd best player in the world. Nothing unsurprising happened in that game either. It was a fair game, and I won through my expected winning condition. I can do this!*

...Unfortunately, Ally ended up taking both of my stocks without dropping any of his. The set was over and he walked away as the victor. I wish I could walk off with the most exciting story saying "iDK beat Ally!" but I'm more than glad to have taken a game despite his ranking and status. It turned out that throughout the entire tournament, he had only lost three games total (from three different people), taking the tournament. Even in grand finals, his opponent was only able to take a single game. It felt pretty good to be one of those three for the day, and it was undoubtedly a powerful motivation for the future to come. Sure, it would have been amazing to have him on my résumé of notable players I've beaten, but at the end of the day, given my current skill at that time, what more could I ask for? Every day, I wonder how the outcome would have been if my mindset, approaching that match, were a bit different. Who knows where I'd be today without that one game win? Without that motivation boost?

Looking for the positives in any situation is, in fact, a skill that can be worked on. Because people rarely see it as a skill, they never try to develop it. Positivity, especially for oneself, is a skill that should be practiced regularly, if not daily, for its power to truly come into effect. Notice the phrase "especially for oneself." It can be easy to support a family member or a friend, but when it comes to taking care of our own mental health, we don't give it the attention it deserves. Your classmate got a bad grade? You'll probably support them by saying something like, "It's okay, you'll do well on the next exam!" If you were the one with the bad grade though? You're probably more likely to think, *I can't believe I failed that test. I'm a failure...*

In a tournament setting, there are several lines you could tell yourself. Maybe you've played against your opponent's character hundreds of times in the past, so you're actually prepared for the match despite the opponent's ranking. Maybe there's someone you would like to win for, whether it's a mentor, friend, or even yourself. Or if you truly believe that you are underprepared, you can view the upcoming match as a chance to learn from the better player. If you lose a game, it's not over! Remember the story about DanM. Remember to narrow your focus not on your emotions over the results, but instead on asking yourself questions as to how to win the next game. Answering those questions will help you into thinking that you do have the tools after all, and as a bonus can give you just enough hope to win the set.

The more you can add positivity to your mindset, the more benefits you'll see in all aspects of your life. People are more likely to connect with positive emotions—nobody truly prefers having pessimistic friends when others are willing to help you along your way. It opens up our minds to ideas, thinking "maybe this *is* possible" instead of shutting down ideas without giving them a chance. It gives us plenty of psychological benefits as we feel more confident and more hopeful about life in general. Smash is just one of those benefits, while also being a fantastic catalyst for this change of mindset that many competitors realize on their own. All the varying topics covered in this chapter—confidence, overthinking, focus, etc.—all benefit from a positivity change. It becomes a dangerously healthy cycle as one shifts their mindset in real life thanks to Smash, then applying their refreshed mindset in Smash thanks to real life, over and over.

Exposure

Unfortunately, simply reading paragraphs doesn't help much if there is no action to follow through, whether it be the previous section or books about the skill you're trying to improve on. The best way to handle pressure situations is simply to put yourself in similar situations as often as possible. If you want to practice your interviewing skills, go apply to multiple jobs just to go through the interview process. Practice with a friend in mock interviews. Record yourself whether you're with a friend or practicing alone (admittedly we all hate recording ourselves the first time, but I'm a witness to its incredible powers). Or maybe an orchestra concert is coming up and you need to practice a solo piece under pressure. Practicing the piece continuously helps, but can you replicate that with an audience? Have a friend listen to your piece. Recording yourself works in this situation as well. Maybe do a push up for every notable mistake your friend catches—or every mistake you catch by yourself if you can be truly honest with yourself. Put something on the line. What about studying for a standardized test, say the SAT or GRE? There's a reason why so many people recommend taking practice exams. While you're taking those practice exams, put yourself in a similar environment to the actual examination. Give yourself the same time limit. Work on a clear desk with zero distractions. Familiarity is key.

In the world of Smash, people overcome pressure in several ways. They attend as many tournaments as possible regardless of the average skill level and size. Tens. Hundreds. Even thousands. The grind becomes a lifestyle. They may also do money matches—two players putting money on the line where the winner takes it all. It may be as little as $1, more commonly $5, but can become as extreme as $1000[6] [7]. Just take note of the laws in your country because this may be seen as illegal gambling. For example, Japan, one of the most notable countries outside of the United States for Smash, enforces this law so strongly that none of the

---

6   One of the few $1000 money matches was recorded here: https://www.youtube.com/watch?v=jH5ApzKlcGU

7   I personally don't recommend going more than $5, if at all, because at that point I believe it just becomes a fight of who gets to keep their ego.

tournaments offer cash prizes unless it is provided by the game developers. When a player enters a tournament, their entry fee is contributed to the prize pot for the top placing players, and some countries including Japan consider that practice as gambling.

Fun fact: a friend from Hawaii offers food on the line instead of money, adding both pressure and fun to the game we play.[8] He calls them "Burger Battles," "Burrito Brawls," and "Soda Scuffles," and he offers food to the opponent if they win, but takes back the offer if they lose so that the opponent has nothing to lose and everything to gain. It's always a fun time.

* * *

For many in the Smash community, they don't realize that they have the willpower to change themselves until they get deep into competing; doing whatever it takes to get to the next level. They realize that whatever decisions they make, they need to do it with confidence believe that it'll work out. They realize that a positive mindset is effectively a requirement for becoming stronger. You'll find lower level players becoming less upset after a loss, realizing later that they need to become accountable for their own losses in order to grow. For the mid- or high-level players, you see them break their plateaus as they continuously thirst for more knowledge, opening their minds to the fact that there is still room to grow despite claiming wins on good players.

The greatest thing about all of this is that you really can replace Smash with any hobby or career you choose to aspire towards, or really anything you do in your daily life. Less competitive communities may not have to deal with losing matches, but the most talented individuals still tend to be much more open-minded and positive, as it's essentially a requirement

---

8   https://www.reddit.com/r/SSBM/comments/6bnitp/ one_player_in_my_region_refuses_to_do_money/

to grow in any skill. People still need to consider all the possibilities, all the combinations, and permutations of any given decision they're trying to make, before moving forward. Countless repetitions of considering these possibilities are what pushes people to their limits, and more often than not, they'll be glad they did.

I hope these past two chapters offered a fair glimpse of how a match goes in the mind of a Smash competitor. Despite it "just being a video game," plenty runs through the player's mind both in and out of the game. We all take the same steps to get to where we want to be; for thousands, it just so happens to be Smash. We all want to improve our lives and reach our goals, whether or not we have a controller in our hands. Whether you choose to join the competition, spectate this upcoming esport, or simply want to continue aspiring toward your own goals, let's all overcome our challenges, together.

Chapter Twelve

Pool Survivor

Smash is all about striving to become a stronger player every day, one step at a time. We strive to become such a strong version of ourselves that we can one day be proud of. Soon we can feel the hours, weeks, months, even years of work all pay off. Personally, I'm still on the grind after over eight years of competitive gaming! When that day arrives—when we win a tournament, beat someone for the first time after dozens of attempts (i.e. a "bracket demon"), or get a win on a top level player—it's an out-of-body experience that I have never felt anywhere else.

Passing or even acing an exam is not quite the same for me. I take my test, and only after a few hours or days do I get back my score. My mind is no longer on solving the problems, and the feelings during the exam evaporate, whether it's an *I-can-do-it* attitude or an *I-hope-this-works* sense of desperation. Oftentimes, I even have an idea of how I performed on the test based on how confident I felt walking out of the classroom. Receiving my score later to find out that I did better than expected can feel great, but only to a certain degree. It often even felt undeserved ("Wow what a curve!", or maybe I had to take some honest guesses and they happened to be correct), or I simply feel relieved ("Phew, I survived."). Even the feelings of receiving my grade at the end of the semester tend to be similar. These feelings often fade in just a few minutes, maybe half an hour tops.

Many office jobs rarely give me the equivalent sense of winning as well, no matter how passionate I am in them. When I'm constantly organizing files or filling out worksheets with no real end goal, it's just a matter of execution. In my engineering positions, that feeling of victory does come more often—when completing a feature, or releasing a build to the customer, for example, but something isn't quite the same. Maybe it's the fact that I'm getting a paycheck for this (and that paycheck is *not* dependent on how successful the result is), or that it's a team effort so I can't help but think that our team will reach the end goal eventually.

This isn't to say at all that work or school give a lesser sense of accomplishment, or that the work is less important or difficult—not at all! The main difference between these examples and Smash (and esports, sports, and other forms of competition): the task at hand is fighting against you, adapting to your every move. The sense of urgency, that any time in a match can become a make-it-or-break-it moment. The demand to give it your absolute best in every given second. The unknown factor; not knowing how the end will turn out. These sensations are what competitors try to explain what it's like to feel alive. As competitors, we're all addicted to it. That's what we're passionate for, what we live for. It's more than just pressing buttons on a screen. It's the victories we earn after years of trying to become the best we can be.

In the next two chapters, I'll be sharing a few stories of my own victories. This isn't quite so much a moment to humble brag (I swear!) as much as it is to demonstrate what the average competitor feels in their finest moments. These victories have kept me motivated to continue chasing my dream of being the best person and player I can be and to keep playing the game and franchise I love, no matter what obstacles come in my way.

* * *

Major tournaments are tough. For the majority including myself, surviving the first round of pools is a significant accomplishment in itself. This feat is usually reserved only for players whom others throughout the nation have heard of, e.g. those who are power ranked in a high-level region. Usually, only ten to fifteen percent of the total entrants survive past pools, which shows how much better than the average competition you need to be. This is often just as difficult as to winning a weekly tournament, if not even more difficult depending on how the best player in your region fares against the world.

I mentioned surviving pools a few chapters back at EVO 2015, but that tournament, despite its prestige, had a set of rules that no other tournament after would use. Remember how Donkey Kong was nicknamed the Avatar, with several of his attacks wielding multiple elements? Those moves weren't allowed anymore after 2015, since after that tournament, those moves, or "custom moves," were generally considered unbalanced, with Donkey Kong being a notable culprit. As such, the majority exclude their results of that tournament as a part of their Smash résumé in casual conversation, including myself (though that definitely does not lessen the experiences shared there). That said, placing top eight or sixteen in that tournament is still no slouch.

My first time surviving pools, this time with standard rules, occurred on August 2016 at the second anniversary of "Super Smash Con" dedicated to the entire Smash series, held in Chantilly, Virginia. They had everything you could hope for as a dedicated Smash fan, whether you were a regular competitor or a casual spectator who hadn't touched the game since elementary school. For those who didn't enter tournaments, there were so many activities going on—more than any other tournament in the nation. You could visit dozens of talented creatives in the artist alley. You could sit in and listen to panelists talk about topics ranging from how to leverage YouTube as a Smasher to organizing your own Smash events for charity. You could watch people participate in a combo contest where players would perform the most creative strings of attacks upon a defenseless computer opponent, or even enter that contest yourself if you've practiced enough for it. Bands and ensembles would perform all kinds of Nintendo music on a grand stage. In the corner of the venue were several indie games that anyone could try out at no charge. An arcade stood nearby with those huge coin-operated machines with the classics including the first Donkey Kong, also for free. There was even a cosplay contest to bring in non-gamers who still love the Nintendo series. It was a wonderful convention that all other tournaments should try to replicate when it comes to side events, and it only gets better every year.

For competitors, the convention held a tournament for every iteration of Smash: the original for the Nintendo 64 (titled simply "Super Smash Bros." but unofficially referred to as "Smash 64" or "64"), Melee, Brawl, Wii U, and even Project M. Doubles (two versus two) tournaments were held for each game as well, meaning ten brackets were running that entire weekend. Every event was run well and on time, with plenty of time between each wave to play friendlies, ample space around each station, and a generous number of consoles for each tournament. The scheduling of these tournaments was also spread well across three days, with no player ever feeling overwhelmed by time.

For the Smash 4 singles tournament, over 1,200 entrants fought their way to the golden trophy. I was scheduled to play at noon on Friday. With it starting later in the day, I had spent two hours or so beforehand simply playing as many players as possible. There were so many competent players in this region, and I felt so fortunate to have been getting such consistent, great practice. Despite the status of the players I played (many of them being ranked within their region, whether they were from Virginia or a nearby state), I was winning more than I was losing. I would still, however, have to work for each win, constantly coming up with creative ways to bait my opponents into leaving themselves open.

12 P.M. arrived and I walked over to my pool. Oddly my first opponent did not show up, so I was immediately sent to round 2. Yet... even my second opponent didn't show up. While these two freebies were great for my standings, this meant that the first opponent I would actually fight was guaranteed to be a solid player who had already beaten two others. Although I waited about half an hour until I got to play, my hands were still feeling warm from playing the entire day. I started scouting on the matches playing, as there wasn't much else for me to do without leaving the area and risking a forfeit. The average level of the play I was seeing was frankly bringing my confidence up, though I knew "average" didn't mean anything. I didn't need to beat just average—I needed to beat everyone.

I started my first match with my trusted Donkey Kong. My opponent picked an uncommon but competent character, Greninja, a frog ninja from the Pokémon series. There were no Greninjas whom I played around my level in San Diego, nor did I fight against any earlier that day, so I was going in with less experience than desired, hoping my theory and given knowledge of the character would carry me through. He played exactly how Greninja is expected to be played: shooting water shurikens to safely open up my defenses, then going in with literally ninja speed and landing deadly combos once he found himself an opening. Despite fighting against a common strategy, he destroyed my Donkey Kong, taking away both of my stocks without losing any of his. My lack of experience showed in that game, and I wouldn't be surprised if everybody watching agreed.

The second game became a Pokémon battle as I switched to my secondary, Pikachu. He had always been my secondary character since the beginning of my Smash career in Brawl, but he was considered a secondary frankly for good reason. In this next game I was playing in a similar way to my opponent: throwing out projectiles via small lightning jolts that would travel along the stage, then putting significant damage from each combo once I find an opening. I managed to win the second game with a comfortable lead. In the third and final game, he was adapting to my playstyle, but at the moment I could not figure out how I could switch my strategy up against this character. As both sides continued on with the same strategy, the game became a last-hit situation. I threw the frog offstage, where Greninja becomes most vulnerable, as his recovery move does not flinch anyone in its path. Abusing this fact, when he got close to the ledge, I secured a hit that made him ricochet off the stage (called a "stage spike") into the bottom death zone. With skilled timing, one is able to break their momentum when hitting the stage (called a "wall tech" or "stage tech"[1]) and easily get back on stage in an advantageous position, so with that in mind and with the fact that he missed it, I sighed a great exhale that probably lasted an entire five seconds.

I immediately had to play my next opponent, a Diddy Kong main. Although Diddy Kong is considered to be one of Donkey Kong's possibly top five worst matchups (due to Diddy Kong's speed, mobility, and power of controlling a sizable portion of the stage), I was more comfortable

---

1   According to the Smash Wiki page for "techs" (https://www.ssbwiki.com/tech), this term originates from "technical" or "tech hit" awarded in the Street Fighter series for canceling out the effects of certain attacks.

fighting Diddy Kong with Donkey Kong than Pikachu, so alas it became a showdown of the Kong family. I played rather defensively in this match, baiting Diddy Kong into committing first, despite Diddy Kong having the better tools to do the same. We played on a stage called Smashville where a floating platform would move back and forth above the main stage, and I spent majority of the set forcing Diddy Kong to attack me from there. Any time my opponent knocked me off the platform, he would put on as much damage as he could, and he was actually quite proficient at dealing such damage. Fortunately for me, he was only able to successfully launch me off that platform about three times throughout two games; I managed to follow up almost every other attempt with a notable counterattack.

I reported the score to the pool captain, "2–0 iDK." He responded, "You won? That's a really good win. Great job!" That Diddy was an upcoming player that was allegedly close to becoming ranked in Virginia (and has been a few times since the upcoming year). The pool captain continued: "By the way, you're in winner's finals. Win or lose, you both get to continue in bracket tomorrow. Congrats dude!" I hid my excitement in my response, "Oh that's cool, thanks," as if it were easy for me. Although I was supposed to play my pool's winner's finals match, I told the pool captain that I would go to the restroom for a minute. I didn't actually need to use the toilet; I just had to stop myself from shaking, knowing that this was the first time I made it this far in a major tournament. My hands were shaking. My arms were shaking. My whole body was shaking as it almost literally could not contain the excitement. I forced myself to use the urinal, thinking through some odd rationale that I could pee out this elated state. I drank as much water as I could out of the nearest water fountain thinking I could wash down the excitement in my stomach. Irrational thoughts don't mean much when your hard work over the span of multiple years is finally paying off—yet at the same time, it's not even close to over. I could go so much further.

My winner's finals opponent was another Diddy Kong, but this time he was at that time a top 5 ranked player from Georgia, home of two players who have been officially ranked as top 50 players in the world. None of that mattered though. I knew I just had to figure out the task at hand. Beat the Diddy Kong, the same way I just did against my last opponent. Let's see what happens.

I won game one. He had honestly outplayed me most of that game, having done almost twice as much damage as I had done to him, but he had an unfortunate misinput that cost him an early stock. Regardless, in the gaming community, we have a phrase for moments like this: "We take those." Although I was one game away from making it out of pools on the winner's side, I knew that game one was a fluke. I even remember shaking my head right after I won, so I readjusted my strategy, switching up between the same defensive play and going in aggressively.

He destroyed me. He claimed both of my stocks when I claimed none. The outcome of each exchange in game two was similar to game one, despite my change in strategy. Maybe my Donkey Kong wasn't quite ready to take on a Diddy Kong of this caliber, so I decided to try out my Pikachu in game three. I heard him say to himself, "Uh-oh," knowing that Pikachu was a much more competent character. In addition, I was able to play on Pikachu's best stage, since the loser of the latest game gets to pick the stage. Despite these facts, I was never comfortable fighting Diddy Kong as Pikachu, but I tried to make the most of his trepidation.

He changed up his playstyle completely, trying to play as evasively as possible. He capitalized on my playing aggressively in trying to catch him, which in hindsight isn't how Pikachu players normally fight Diddy Kong. Pikachu players usually make the Diddy Kong approach them as the monkey jumps, walks, and shields his way through those tiny electrifying projectiles. I hadn't played enough of Pikachu vs. Diddy Kong at that time to execute that well. Even with my aggressive play, it was still quite a long match that lasted about four to five minutes (a typical game lasts between two to three minutes). He slowly chipped in damage over time, and he eventually won the game, the set, and the pool.

I was fine with this since I still made it out as well. After I talked to a nearby friend who was watching my match, I remember the last thing I told him in that conversation was "It's fine, I still made it out of pools!" and him responding "You right, let's go, iDK!" Not too long after, I happened to see DKwill for the first time that weekend, giving him the good news and in response him giving me an enthusiastic fist bump with a smiling "Let's gooooooo!" I had a sudden flashback to when I had first met him a year and a half ago, contemplating about how much I've grown as a player since then.

I spent a good amount of time after my pool playing even more friendlies. I just wanted to get better and grow as a player, and I had all the resources right around me to do so. I managed to play against the Greninja I fought in my pool for a solid half hour, solidifying my experience against that character, using both Donkey Kong and Pikachu. I kept playing as many players as I could until dinner time finally hit and friends reached out to me to grab food nearby. After dinner, I went straight to my hostel to see who I would play next: a Ryu. Street Fighter versus Pokémon was about to go down as I was prepared to go in with Pikachu, whom Ryu players consider to be one of their toughest matchups. I tried looking up a bit more information about my opponent after, assuming I won, but I couldn't find any information about them. That might have been a good thing as I could focus on studying just one character. By the end of the night, I had watched about eight different matches of Pikachu versus Ryu, analyzing every exchange and how they happened. I wrote up about five pages of notes and started resting up for the next day.

Saturday was a repeat of Friday for me: play a bunch of friendlies until my bracket, but instead, this day's bracket was at 2 P.M. instead of noon. I skimmed through my notes about ten minutes beforehand. The gist of my notes were saying: Pikachu can die as early as 30%, so don't do anything risky; make Ryu come to you, and run around him since Pikachu easily outspeeds Ryu; keep crouching and crawling because none of Ryu's aerials are safe against a low profile; and if you have ANY doubt that a move is guaranteed to connect in time, don't risk it. Ryu is a heavy character who is likely to survive past 150% against Pikachu, whereas Pikachu is the exact opposite. Regardless of what percent Ryu was at, I was never winning until I secured the stock. I kept telling myself, *play as safely as possible, play as safely as possible, play as safely as possible.*

He brought out his Ryu as expected. I used my Pikachu as intended. I won the first game solidly without dropping a stock. Despite the results, it wasn't easy. The notes kept scrolling in the back of my mind throughout the entire game, and I made sure not to forget any of those tips at any time. I couldn't drop my guard just yet, as he could figure out my strategy easily the next game. I need to remember that I'm against a living human being—one who made it to this day as well—so he had all the power to adapt to my playstyle. He chose to go back to the same stage. He reverses the roles, claiming both of my stocks without dropping any of his. Oh. I thought to myself, maybe I was playing *too* defensively or at least defensively with a pattern too obvious. 1–1 now, but I had a slight advantage at this point not only because of the character choice but also due to my being able to choose the final stage (the loser of the previous game picks the next game' stage).

Game three comes around, and we're on Final Destination, a stage with zero platforms. We suddenly had an audience of four to five people. I ended up getting into a bad situation: I was at 50% at the corner, and he was at around 150%, both on our last tournament stock. Higher percent means they've taken more damage, right? Yes, but remember, Ryu doesn't care about percents. Higher percents to him just means he can kill earlier (remember rage and Ness's PK Thunder 2). Remember the notes—30% meant death percent for Pikachu. The percentage in this game didn't mean less health; it meant fewer opportunities. Since I was in the corner with limited options, he was actually the one winning via positioning. Even though I was only a third of his percent, we were both one hit away from death.

I managed to get back to the center of the stage unscathed, trapping him in the corner. Ryu had no room to move backward. All the power seemed to be in my control, but we were both visibly shaking. I literally felt the shaking in the floor's vibrations. He wasn't planning on moving in, despite all the projectiles I was throwing at him. He was waiting for me to commit to something, and he wanted to punish me for it. It all made sense, with the way he was shaking and how his character would stay in the corner.

I took a deep breath and trusted my instincts. I let go of all hesitation. I went in. I juked out an aerial attack by just hopping close to him, but not completely in his face. He threw out a Shoryuken—a jumping uppercut that starts off with invincibility. This undoubtedly would have killed if it connected, but just as I had planned, it didn't. and I punished his landing as Ryu is completely vulnerable from after he throws that attack until he lands. I throw out my final blow using Pikachu's "up smash," a powerful backflip using Pikachu's head to send them to the sky. I moved on in bracket.

It literally could have gone either way. If he suddenly walked a bit forward and then followed up with the Shoryuken, I was dead. If he did a horizontally ranged attack instead, I probably would have survived but I would have been shaking even more since I would be in a worse position with an even higher percentage. I may still have lost, but just with my death delayed. We gave each other the firmest, sweatiest handshakes ever, and I fell into my seat almost hyperventilating. A few people cheered for me, "Let's GO!" I couldn't look around, as I was just trying to catch my breath. The win felt even more powerful than making it out of pools. *Oh my gosh, oh my gosh, oh my gosh, I'm STILL in this.* All the studying paid off, but unfortunately, I had no idea what was coming up next.

It turns out that my next opponent was watching that match since he was waiting for the winner, but I knew he now had information on my playstyle whereas I had nothing on him—not even his character. Regardless, I felt like my Pikachu was playing on point, so I stuck with him onto our next match. He ended up using Samus, a projectile-heavy character from the *Metroid* series. I had zero experience with a Samus at this level. Fortunately for me, Pikachu is known to be one of Samus's worst matchups just like Ryu, but just like the previous set, I knew that now was not the time to relax.

My opponent imitated my Donkey Kong's playstyle versus the Diddy Kongs. He would run toward the Smashville platform and charge a powerful energy shot. I couldn't figure out how to get in. If I approached him head-on, he would shoot me with a giant shot—a shot as big as Donkey Kong—dealing a whopping 25%. He could unleash the shot at any time, even if it weren't fully charged. If I approached from above, he would use his instantaneous Screw Attack (an incredibly fast get-off-my option, however with a wide opening for punishment if it misses) to keep me away. And if I tried to approach from a diagonal, he would use his grapple beam (Samus's "zair" for the Smash players here). While this grapple beam would be quite weak, it extends about four to five times the length of Samus herself. All these threats proved Samus to be a formidable character for me to fight against, and my opponent clearly knew his character well. "Pikachu is known to be one of Samus's worst matchups" didn't mean much if players didn't know how to take full advantage of the reasoning behind this, and admittedly I was nowhere near as comfortable as I could have been.

I won the first game, albeit barely, catching a defensive roll when we were both a hit away from death. My opponent secured game two, having played even more defensively. In game three I decided to go back to the same stage one last time, knowing that I had already won a game there. History repeated itself as Samus once again started by retreating to the platform and charging. This time, I stayed diagonally underneath her, waiting for her to commit first. Being under an opponent is generally an advantageous position in Smash, so I was not willing to give that up. However, whenever Samus decided to drop down from the platform, I couldn't quite get my hands on her. She even landed a few hits on me along the way day. Both sides repeated this strategy and my opponent eventually took my stock first. This match dragged on for a full four minutes before a single stock was lost that game. I instinctively let go of my controller and brought my arm in, shaking my fist. I knew this was still possible.

Unfortunately, time was ticking, and my opponent knew it. There was only one minute left on the timer, and he had a significant lead. In Smash, when a timeout occurs, the game will bring itself into a sudden death mode if both players are at equal stocks, but competitive Smash ignores this sudden death mode. The winner instead would be determined by who has the lesser percent, if not the greater number of stocks. As such, at the given rate I was going to lose. Knowing that, I went in aggressively hoping for the best since admittedly I wasn't sure what else to do with that little time left. His defenses were too much for me as he shot at me right as I got in his face, and I lost my final tournament stock of the weekend.

My intensity slowly faded as I gave him a solid handshake, complimenting his playstyle and patience in an unfavorable matchup. My run was over, but all the raw emotions running throughout the two days made it probably my most enjoyable tournament of the year. I ended up placing 97th out of 1,272 entrants. My crew and friends from Hawaii were proud of my run as they were peeking at the online brackets, messaging me about how the whole experience was. Out of everyone in my crew, I had been the first person to make it out of pools at a major tournament (although each person in my crew had entered at most only one or two tournaments of this scale), so they kept applauding me for representing the crew and Hawaii. Although they were 5,000 miles away, it felt like they were right beside me at the moment.

Now, all there was left to do was to enjoy the convention. I left the tournament area to watch the symphonic band open up their first piece (with such coincidental timing): the Super Smash Bros. Melee opening theme. They even had a choir which made the song even more incredible. The choir ended the theme the same way the game would: echoing throughout the entire hall, "SUPER SMASH BROTHERS... MELEE!" The combination of goosebumps from the music with what I was still feeling from my tournament run solidified my passion: no matter what obstacles came in the way, I could never give up Smash. Not with all the friends that come with it, the growth as an individual, realizing I have the potential to become one of the best players out there, and after that day knowing what it feels like to be alive when I'm giving everything I've got.

Chapter Thirteen

My Time to Shine

There have been countless times when I've gotten close, but I could never close out the final stock. Against ranked people in San Diego, ranked players in Southern California, even against top 10 players in the entire world. This tends to be seen as frustrating, knowing that I was so close yet in the end, this is worth as much of a loss as not doing a single percent of damage. I tend to see it in a more positive light, knowing that I'm on the right track and with enough time, practice, and experience, I'll get to where I want to be soon.

One of the most monumental days of my time playing Smash happened at the second anniversary of New England's premiere tournament, "Shine 2017" in late August at Boston, Massachusetts. People often mention both Super Smash Con and this tournament in their top five tournament experiences of all time, and I would have to agree. Everything was run efficiently even while the staff was managing over a dozen brackets, including non-Smash games. There was plenty of space, over 50 setups, and hundreds of seats to watch streamed matches. The artist alley had a plethora of art pieces to sell, as did many other sponsored vendors. Most importantly for the competitors, Shine ran a side event "Lane Shift" where you sign up for as many brackets, or "lanes," as you wish. Which lane you end up in was determined by your placing in the main bracket as well as how many Lane Shift brackets you've won. With tons of swag as prizes, most would still try to play their best, and thus this would help players level up quickly in an entertaining way. This concept kept competitors motivated to play even right after they've been eliminated from the standard bracket (at most events, competitors unfortunately typically leave the venue for the rest of the day, discouraged).

In addition to all the activities happening at this event, the players of New England were one of the most passionate people in the community as well. You could hear cheering and shouting everywhere throughout the venue, especially during top 8. I still keep in touch with the people I met here more than most regions I've traveled to, simply due to how amicable they all are on top of their energetic personalities. Pair all this with the abundance of what Boston has to offer—especially the food!—and you've got fans who can't wait to come again the next year.

Boston was one of the most anticipated cities that I could not wait to visit for the first time, mostly because of the lobster and clam chowder that awaited my stomach. I've always been an avid seafood fan—one of my uncles actually owned a Chinese seafood restaurant, so many of our family dinners came with crab and lobster, even when I was three years old. With that said, on this trip, I was ecstatic from the moment I left my home. I was simply in a fantastic mood the entire time, which may have helped my mentality when competing. I was more excited about this trip than any other. Usually, I would more so be curious instead of what the city had to offer.

I arrived in the city on Thursday morning after a red-eye across the country. I decided to fly in a full day before the tournament so I could give the city the attention it deserves (I try to do this with every city), and I knew there was a *lot* to do in Boston. Despite traveling alone, I was loving every moment of that day. I hit up the beautiful campuses of Harvard and MIT, wandered around downtown and Chinatown, walked along the historic Freedom Trail as it explained the history of the nation, strolled along the pier, enjoyed the fresh air of the Boston Common park, and devoured amazing chowder at the Faneuil Hall Marketplace, all with the perfect summer weather in late August. I had probably walked a full ten miles in that one day, as I remember in *Pokémon Go* hatching three eggs, heh. Pokémon Go makes sightseeing so much more enjoyable than it already is thanks to all the PokéStops sharing valuable real-life information in the game, and of course with catching all the Pokémon along the way.

The most significant part of my day, however, was when I simply went out for lunch that day. A friend of mine who had visited the city before recommended me to try out a certain ramen shop, as it was an experience one would never get anywhere else. *What could be so special about a ramen shop?* I asked myself (having forgotten to ask my friend about it), despite ramen being one of my top five favorite foods of all time. Even all the reviews on Yelp were calling it an experience, but I couldn't quite relate to what they were all saying until I went there myself.

The ramen shop, Yume Wo Katare, was just a five-minute bus ride away from Harvard, the first place I was exploring for the day. I arrived about half an hour before they were closing, so there wasn't much of a wait. The entire line got in within ten minutes, and my eyes couldn't help but wander around what the quaint little shop had to offer. We were each told where to sit among one of three rows of wooden benches; each row could only fit about five people. More customers would only come in, five at a time, whenever a bench emptied out. A large poster hung on the wall, reading "What's your purpose in life?" Surrounding that poster laid dozens of colored index cards with people's hopes and dreams written on them. While these hopes and dreams varied in intensity (from "acing my next test" to "to explore all seven continents!"), the wall felt alive as I could feel the energy within each person's handwriting.

The menu had only two food items on it: a regular pork ramen bowl and a large one. After seeing the images on Yelp, I ordered the regular-sized one due to how enormous it already is; many reviews on the website claimed normally ordering large portions at most restaurants but having to resort to a regular size here. After everybody in the row ordered, the owner of the restaurant (with only one other employee in the shop cooking up the food) shared with us his vision: a social atmosphere where people can be open to sharing their beautiful dreams with each other. The owner shared his own dream of opening up this shop, as well as one in Japan, which encouraged the customers to share their own dreams if they wanted to. He also explained that your dreams will come true if you're able to complete your meal, soup and all, without taking any home. With that said, customers couldn't have their phones out while eating so that they could truly appreciate the food and concentrate on making their dreams a reality.

The meal itself was heavy, not only in sheer quantity but in the amount of garlic and oil added to the broth. The pork itself was covered in fat but in a shamefully delicious way. The entire bowl was more of a guilty pleasure than ramen usually is, but I was determined to finish it. Halfway through the bowl, I was starting to slow down already, but at that point, I decided to share my short-term dream with the store. "I'm visiting Boston this weekend to compete in a video gaming competition, so all I wish for is to perform my best while I'm here." The customers cheered, saying how cool that dream was. People started asking questions, "What game?" "What character do you use?" "Can I watch it online?" The entire store, owner included, started sharing a conversation about esports, something I never would have imagined with strangers, especially since I was probably the second- or third-youngest person there. I felt a bit of social anxiety before sharing my dream, but after braving the storm and committing to the store's vision, I was glad I took a chance. Doing so gave me the motivation to finish up the second half of my bowl, although it did take me over twenty minutes to do so. As the owner picked up my dishes and gave me my check, he exclaimed, "PERFECT!" sharing with the restaurant that I had cleared my bowl completely. With other customers, he would shout phrases such as "NEXT TIME!" for those who could not eat everything, or "GOOD JOB!" for those who ate everything but left the broth. I left the restaurant with a unique feeling—more motivated than ever to not necessarily win, but to simply play my heart out, mixed with a stomach so full that I was forced to walk at half my normal speed for the next hour.

* * *

Friday arrived, and thus it was time to head to the venue. The first day of the event ran primarily the doubles brackets. I personally rarely competed in doubles, but at this tournament, I signed up since I was going to compete with an old friend from Houston, Texas, whom I had met almost two years before at MLG Finals in New Orleans. He went by the tag "Daffle" and was one of the friendliest players I had met there. His talent shined in doubles as he could take down teams with top 50 players. His Villager provided fantastic support, as Villager's slingshots prevented the opposing team from getting anything started, while at the same time following up my punishes for incredibly early kills. Moves that would never connect in a one-verse-one setting kept connecting every thirty seconds. Meanwhile, I had to rely more on my general Smash skills, as I didn't specialize in doubles at all. I only knew the basics of doubles that majority of players can't quite execute well: instigate as many two-verse-one situations as you can. Whether this is saving your partner from a combo or simply following up on your partner's throw, these little things all add up if one can remember to do so consistently.

Daffle and I had actually competed in doubles together for the first time just four months before this event at a major in Austin, and we did surprisingly well given no prior doubles practice. At Shine, we ended up with a shorter run, but we played at about the same level as before; it was just that the average level at Shine was much higher, losing to top 50 players as well as power ranked players in New England. Overall it was an enjoyable run, and we both more so felt glad for being able to compete together for a second time.

After our doubles run, I spent the entire rest of the day getting solid practice against new faces in friendlies. I had probably played friendlies for a total of eight hours throughout the entire day. Everyone I met was a pleasure to both talk to and play against. There was not a single person whom I could not perform less than my best against, even people who used one of the worst characters in the game. Most of them also complimented how I used my characters, including my Diddy Kong which replaced my Pikachu at the beginning of 2017 for personal reasons. The switch also made sense given my gamer tag.

They would all ask who the biggest threat is in my pool, and I would respond: "Pugwest." At that time he was ranked third in New England and first in Rhode Island, but his peak was 39th in the world in the second season (July to December 2016) of the top 50 rankings. Pugwest was a wielder of the *Fire Emblem* swordsman Marth, and he was known as one of the best Marth players in the world. Marth was one of the most comfortable characters I enjoyed fighting against using Donkey Kong, so I half-jokingly told my new friends that I could do it. To my surprise, they all wholehearted replied in one way or another, "I believe it dude." I've never appreciated a sentiment so much before.

The next day, I had never felt so ready. Since I had a late pool at 4 P.M., I ended up waking up as late as 10 A.M. The hostel I was staying at provided free breakfast, so I indulged in what I didn't know at that time my last meal before my bracket run. My hostel was also located within the heart of Chinatown, so I grabbed a bubble tea, my staple pre-tournament drink whenever it was available, and headed my way to the venue.

I had about five more hours until my pool. What else to do? Keep practicing of course! I played a few of the same people from the day before, and I was somehow playing even better. I started winning games consistently when I would previously win slightly more than half of them. It was only the beginning of the day too. My hands would warm up so much more over the upcoming hours, and muscle memory would click in so much more easily. I was easily beating people whom I called amazing just the day before. I didn't want to give this idea too much thought, but perhaps my experience with the ramen shop was actually giving me the power boost I needed.

4 P.M. arrived, and I could not be any more ready. I was the first person called by the pool captain. A mere five minutes later, her eyes widened up as I reported the score. I don't think I have ever won a tournament set so quickly, and my first opponent was not too bad at all. I was told to stay at my seat, and she called Pugwest to my station.

We play game one on Smashville, the stage with the single moving platform. He played both aggressively yet patiently, staying in front of my face the entire time but not necessarily always swinging. He knew more often than not when to fully commit, and he would juggle me in the air constantly, something Marth does notably well. Donkey Kong is also one of the weakest characters in the game when he's above his opponent, and Pugwest undoubtedly knew that, pushing his advantage as far as he could to the point where I lost a stock without making it back to the ground a single time. He ended up taking both of my stocks cleanly, whereas I had only taken one without doing much damage on his second. I shrugged it off, however. I knew that in the end, he really only held advantageous positions about three times that game—he just knew how to push that position well. If I can change that number from three to two, or even less, I could turn the set around.

In the second game, I took him to Final Destination, the stage with no platforms. Game two started similarly, where I get a few stray hits here and there, but every hit he landed led to solid juggling. Before I knew it, I was above 150%, and he was only at 50%. I was taking every hit that looked like a finishing blow, but I kept on surviving. I realized then that I was playing more passively than usual, so once I got back to the center of the stage I would play more aggressively, fighting fire with fire. He ends up missing an aerial attack, and I grab him upon his landing. Donkey Kong's most notable combo is that at certain percents, his grab leads to a vertical kill by throwing the opponent up in the air, followed by an upward headbutt. Normally, this would kill Marth starting around 80%, but with the rage mechanic and me being above 150%, I secured the first kill, even though he had dealt twice the damage I did. On paper, it may sound quite unfair, but Smash 4 is truly more a game of opportunities than a game of percentages and numbers. While for the most part, you will have more opportunities when your opponent is at a higher percent, opportunities can open up at the earliest percents, and it is up to both the aggressor for seizing the opportunity as well as the defender for avoiding said opportunity. Life itself shares this same sentiment, which causes many to claim life to be unfair. For example, college does not guarantee careers in the field but provides more opportunities for one to do so. Conversely, people who don't even finish high school can make riches with motivation and the right resources, and perhaps a bit of luck.

Upon respawning, Pugwest used the few seconds of invincibility granted on a new stock to secure his first kill of the game on me. The game was now even, with both of us on our fresh second stock. The second stock moved at a similar pace, despite my attempt to change my playstyle and move around more. We ended up in the same situation with me above 150% and him at 50% again. Things were starting to look grim, but I kept telling myself, *as long as he doesn't hit me with a solid kill move, I'll be fine.* I knew what moves he was looking to kill with, so all I had to avoid were those specific moves. It was still okay to get hit by weaker moves, so with that rationale I was able to calm myself down just a bit. I didn't have to avoid *everything.* He eventually got me offstage, but he didn't have enough time to jump off and hit me so he stayed near the ledge. As I grabbed the ledge, I hung on there to see if he would throw out any preemptive attack. He guessed that I would come back onto the stage aggressively, doing whatever it would take to turn the tables around, so he held up his shield in preparation to counterattack. Noticing that he was holding this shield for a while, I went for it all with Donkey Kong's side special: a shield-breaking headbutt. It was a risky move on my part. I would have been dead if he had let go of his shield to attack before my headbutt, which is slower than almost all of Donkey Kong's attacks. Fortunately, everything ended up in my favor, and so I fully charged Donkey Kong's strongest attack and secured game two with the victory.

At the moment, I honestly didn't feel like I deserved that game. After all, he did deal about twice as much damage as me. It was fine though, as nothing mattered except for the numbers we would tell the pool captain. I tried to justify the win: I was able to survive every hit, and I took advantage of the game mechanics. I had to remind myself, *I took the opportunity presented to me, and I went with it.* While the justification didn't seem enough to me and I couldn't get rid of the guilt of winning that game, I also knew that I could redeem myself in this final game. I still had a chance to change up my playstyle just enough to net the biggest win of my Smash career thus far. I also knew from Pugwest's facial expressions that he felt like he unfairly lost that game, showing an obvious disdainful, unamused face. He eventually shrugged with the expression of "It is what it is," trying to keep his cool.

In game three, he took me to Lylat Cruise, a stage with slants on the edges and three floating platforms close to the main stage. I noticed that he started playing more passively, allowing me to start my first string of attacks. I juggled him just as well as he did to me prior, using the platforms to trap his landings, as there is a bit of lag whenever one lands on a surface. This eventually led me to Donkey Kong's grab to kill combo at around 80%. I got a few stray hits here and there on his second stock, but he reversed the juggling once again to take away my first stock. I still had a lead, so all was fine in my mind.

With my new stock invincibility, I started juggling him again. He couldn't get down at all; my ability to trap his landings were on point. I kept hitting him back up into the air, and he had no jumps left to get out of the situation. He eventually tried to land diagonally from me in an attempt to swing an aerial attack, in which I knew it was time. I let out Donkey Kong's most popular attack as powerful as it has ever been from the beginning of Smash: a fully charged Giant Punch. Dealing a whopping 28% on top of the 80% he had, the attack sent him all the way to the corner of the screen. Marth had stayed in the corner for a while as if he had barely survived the hit, but soon enough our eyes laid upon the one word everyone but Pugwest was looking for: "GAME!"

We both gave each other a firm handshake, both of us with the sweatiest of hands. He stood up, and asked me, "Where are you from?" I told him I was a dual Hawaii-SoCal resident. He had the tiniest smirk, "Makes sense," as he reported to the pool captain from where he stood, then walked off to wait for his loser's run. It took me about a full minute to get out of my seat, taking in what just happened. I turned around and see a few guys I played friendlies earlier that day and the day before. "I knew you could do it, dude." "Clutchest win ever!" "That's a REALLY good win!" I was so appreciative of these comments, especially as they were coming from these New England residents talking about me taking down one of their heroes—and they're known for their regional pride.

I was feeling a mixture of disbelief, ecstasy, and power. *I can't believe I did it. I DID IT. NOBODY can get in my way now.* I felt like hopping all over the venue and just running around to let all my energy out. There was just *so* much energy flowing throughout my body. That whole moment was truly ineffable. I'd ridden the world's steepest roller coaster in Japan, skydived in Hawaii, and even run a marathon, but all of those activities were nothing compared to this. The excitement that comes from fulfilling a goal you never thought you would actually accomplish? It's a feeling no school or job could ever replicate—a feeling that only competition could provide. That excitement makes people feel alive. That excitement makes people feel like life is worth living

But wait! I still had the rest of my bracket to go through. I told my next opponent I had to calm down first—he empathized with the feelings I was going through—and so just like at Super Smash Con I headed to the restroom. I practically skipped my way there with my water bottle, filled it up all the way in the bathroom sink since there were no nearby water fountains, and immediately drank about 20 ounces to calm myself down. I then started pacing around in circles, still trying to calm my excitement, since I knew playing with any kind of emotion, good or bad, would be disruptive to my play. It didn't matter that I pulled the biggest Smash win of my life at that moment because I still needed to compete right then and there. I took about ten minutes to return to my opponent, but he didn't mind at all. I finally sat down, and we started our match.

He had been watching a bit of my match against Pugwest, so he started off with Rosalina and Luma, a duo consisting of a princess and a living star from the Mario universe. More importantly, this was undoubtedly Donkey Kong's worst matchup. This was even considered to be one of the worst matchups in the entire game. If both players are of equal skill level, the Donkey Kong is known to almost never win this match. This was such an unfavorable matchup for Donkey Kong that when I use Rosalina for fun, whom I almost never play with, she could effortlessly take down my fellow Donkey Kong brethren. Rosalina was the primary reason why going solo with Donkey Kong in bracket is generally considered unviable. Even DKwill uses other characters for Rosalina.

I destroyed him. No stocks lost.

He wasn't a bad player at all either. After all, he was in round 3 on the winner's side as well, and I was still sweating the entire game. He even ended up in the loser's semifinals round of our pool. I had just stuck with my game plan against Rosalina, knowing that there would be times where I'm forced to play this matchup instead of relying on another character. Momentum was certainly on my side as well.

Regardless of the game one result, I knew I wanted to switch to

Diddy Kong. He switched to Fox, whom he admitted was his primary character at the end of the set, but his Fox was no match for me as well. He was honestly a scary competitor, but somehow I managed to win the set without dropping a stock. The fire within me was uncontrollable—or perhaps it was the ramen.

I was in the winner's finals of my pool. I looked at my phone before my next match and noticed that practically the entire Smash community was congratulating me on my Pugwest win. I put it on airplane mode since I knew now was not the time to celebrate. Next up was the second-ranked player in New Hampshire, a Greninja. Unlike my match at Super Smash Con, my Pikachu was no longer in practice so I couldn't rely on him, but I knew I had learned enough of the nuances of the matchup using Donkey Kong by now. I intended on sticking with the gorilla the entire set, as my experience with Diddy Kong against Greninja was not so great at that time.

He started with the defensive projectile shooting with the water shurikens as expected, but I remained calm the entire time. I tried to block as many as possible, but I didn't mind at all if I missed blocking a few. Each uncharged shuriken that connected would only deal about 2% after all. He, however, tried switching to close-ranged offense often, which I was ready for and punished heavily. The first game was quite a convincing win for me. We both stuck with the same character and stage. He recognized his errors of going in, so he spent the entire match shooting shurikens until I messed up on my defense significantly (such as getting hit by a fully charged shuriken), from which then he would capitalize on. Closing in on the space against these shurikens can be pretty tricky, since Greninja can charge and release them at any moment, and Greninja was incredibly swift as a character. My opponent was mixing up the timing on these projectiles well too. He won game two without dropping a stock.

In game three, I was playing the same defensive game, but this time I would occasionally get hit by the shurikens on purpose so that following up would appear to be safe when it actually wasn't. If he didn't follow up when I purposely got hit, I would still be fine. Taking 2% at a time? No problem. I did successfully land a few hits here and there using my strategy, but none of the hits led to anything substantial. It was a pretty even game throughout until I got the grab to kill combo to take his first stock. However, soon after, he eventually got me offstage and finished my first stock there. On the second stock, he played a bit more aggressively, landing much more damage but with me dealing just as much damage back. His impatience netted him more damage, but at the same time, he left himself open a lot more. The end was looking grim as he started an impressive combo that I couldn't get out of, dealing more than 50% and leading to my death—except that he barely missed his finishing blow. He played recklessly immediately after, frustrated about missing his opportunity, and I turned it around to take the win. Another huge sigh of relief from me as we exchanged even more sweaty hands.

I don't know how, but I ended up lying down on the floor. My body couldn't handle all the emotions, the adrenaline, the relief. I probably ended up just lying there with my eyes shut for a good five minutes. My pool was finally over, and I could finally take a break—at least for an hour. I grabbed my phone and turned off airplane mode, reading upon a plethora of tweets congratulating me. The Twitter account that handled the official worldwide rankings, "PGStats," was tweeting live about Shine's upsets, and there it was: "iDK > Pugwest."[1] That's all that needed to be said. I made a simple tweet of my own informing my followers out of sheer ecstasy, and sure enough, my phone started to

---

1   https://twitter.com/ThePGstats/status/901545998119444480

vibrate even more. People were retweeting both tweets, and top players I hadn't met liked it. Twitter became my virtual celebration party. My phone was constantly vibrating throughout the rest of the day. Of course, I didn't want to put the tweet's conversations on mute! I was basking in the glory, for who knows when this would ever happen again.

Everything that happened after pools? My momentum notably faltered, and so... let's not talk about that. But I didn't really mind. I placed 65th out of 659 entrants, with a notable win to add on my Smash resume. Reaching the top level actually looked possible now. There was nothing more I could do to boost that placing, so all I could do was appreciate how far I've gotten.

...and play more friendlies and competing in the Lane Shift side brackets for the rest of the day. Only until the venue was about to close for the night, around 10 P.M., did I realize that I hadn't eaten anything all day, so I grabbed a nice seafood dinner nearby along the harbor to commemorate myself for the day. When I went back to the hostel after, I couldn't help but stay awake on my phone until around 4 A.M. chatting with friends, responding to tweets, and thinking about what in the world just happened in the past twelve hours. I kept shaking in my bed, all in sheer excitement. I had probably thought to myself, *Today did not just happen*, about a dozen times every five minutes for five hours straight. When I did fall asleep, it was the most restful night I have had in a long time—probably since the time I ran a full marathon, three years before. *So, this is what bliss feels like.*

* * *

By the end of Smash 4's lifespan, I had quite a résumé for my Smash career that I couldn't be prouder of. Smash 4 had only lasted four years, but the journey was incredible. I may not have grown as fast as others, but these years were the greatest ride of my life. I had my highest highs.

I had my lowest lows. My years in high school were substantially easier, both academically and emotionally. Even college, despite the workload I had, barely left a dent on me emotionally. In Smash, however, I kept falling short, for years, but every now and then I would net a decent win to pick myself back up. Traveling across the country to only win a single set couldn't be more devastating. Not winning any matches at a weekly tournament when I was expected to place within the top half felt just as discouraging. I had felt like quitting the game multiple times, but I knew that quitters never win. At the same time, no matter what the results said, my heart could never let go of this game, so the only choice left was to pull myself together and work even harder.

Little did I know at that time, I've experienced far more failures than successes, but perhaps those successes wouldn't feel like successes if it weren't for those failures. I thought I had accomplished quite a bit at that point in my life outside of Smash, but while they may look impressive to others, they never felt as big of accomplishments as the ones I reached in Smash. Making it out of Super Smash Con pools felt better than getting my first college 4.0 (and that semester contained all engineering classes). Beating Pugwest felt more powerful to me than completing a marathon. In hindsight, I'm so glad that I failed so many times. Without them, reaching my goals wouldn't feel like they were worth achieving.

As Smash 4 was coming to a close, so was this chapter of my life. While I may have conquered dozens of my goals throughout this time, many more await for me in Ultimate. There was so much more in store for me. In Smash 4, I peaked on San Diego's power ranking at 9th, getting on for the first time in the summer of 2018. How much further could I go on San Diego's power ranking? Can I make it onto SoCal's power ranking? Could I become a national threat? Could I become known as one of the innovating pioneers of my character? Would I be sticking with Donkey Kong along my journey through Ultimate? What other characters would accompany me as I strive to reach the top? I couldn't be more ready.

Chapter Fourteen

The Smash Career

Throughout this book, I've been using the term "Smash career" as referring to one's journey through Smash as they strive to reach the top, whether they're a hobbyist or professional. However, wrapping up this story, I've discovered that the number of parallels to one's "real-life" career... is rather uncanny. I love the implications that come with this term. It's made me approach every individual I meet in life in a new light: of empathy and curiosity. There's just so much depth to this sense of wonder, with the unlimited back story to every individual's Smash career, with all the life lessons we've all learned on our own through this love-hate relationship we call Smash.

Rarely anyone ever joins the competitive Smash scene initially thinking, *I want to become a professional Smash player.* One usually just checks out a local tournament after playing casually with friends for the longest time, followed by *I got bodied...* Sometimes this gets paired with the desire to do better next time, but that path surely is not for everyone. This desire, as most newcomers don't realize until it's too late, is surprisingly addicting. Many share an experience similar to my own and all that I've described in this book. Next thing they know, it's one of the most important parts of their lives as they live every day grinding to be better than they were the day before. All of this may just be for a video game, but all the hard work put into this game is no different than into any other passion. That dedication makes us feel alive, especially when we realize and reap the fruits of our labor.

Each Smash competitor has their own story. Every person has their own crew of partners to train with, who got them to where they are today. Every person has put in countless hours—literally thousands—honing their craft, perfecting their technical execution, ensuring that they can pull off their combos perfectly under pressure. Every person has dedicated themselves to analyzing their play, learning from other's plays, interpreting the mindset of professional players winning tournaments and replicating it themselves. Many end up traveling out of their region solely to compete, seeing how they fare against the world and proving that all the time, they devoted to this game will eventually be worthwhile. To me, meeting every Smash player becomes so fascinating because of all these factors that I can guarantee they've been through to some degree. For a shy introvert like me, these moments of meeting players from all around the world and actually getting to know them is so beautiful. It becomes easy for people in this community to open up to each other, sharing their successes and failures in this journey we're all in together. And in a way, we all share this same journey called life. Even if I share zero interests with a person I just met outside of Smash, every person has their own story to share.

I wish every human being could put in as much love and effort into their passion as dedicated Smash players do. I love seeing people trying to make something out of their lives, trying to leave their mark in society, trying to make the world a better place through their own means. I love aspiring actors working their way to Hollywood, artists trying to create art for art's sake, developers trying to create the next movement in technology, medical students studying night and day to save lives. Whatever their passion, whatever their career, I love hearing about it, learning about it, and maybe even trying to apply their practices into my own life in some interdisciplinary way.

Everyone at some point in their career realizes one of life's important lessons that everyone has heard before: balance is key. As much as you want to put your heart into a passion, you can't spend every minute of your life tackling the goal. Many realize that improvement in areas outside of that specific skill is paramount: family, personal growth, health, and fitness, financial growth, social life, character, and integrity, ethics and virtues; the list goes on. Life is a giant balance scale with dozens of weighing pans, and if anything goes off balance, the entire body and mind start to fall apart. All the gears need to be well-oiled for the machine to run optimally, and Smash is no exception. Otherwise, there will be burnout. Fatigue. Stress (and not the good kind). This book, unfortunately, isn't an excuse to play video games 24/7. We've all been there, but I hope this book has helped you in some way to figure out that balance.

Through Smash, I have met the widest spread of individuals. I've met fellow engineers, medical students, musicians, artists, bloggers, educators, veterans, priests, lawyers, bartenders, baristas, middle school students better at the game than I, and so many more. The fact that one shared hobby can lead to limitless backgrounds, each with their own story and aspirations, is so amazing. I could spend my entire life just playing and meeting new Smashers, sharing my stories with them, learning about what they do and how they plan to get there. Oftentimes, I can see a correlation between how their dedication to Smash has impacted their career aspirations, which is incredibly fascinating. Few examples: many in the community have affirmed their desire to excel in graphic design by creating work for their local tournament's needs. Others have made the most of their marketing skills to bring in as many players to their region's biggest tournament. Some have utilized their communications degree to become the next upcoming commentator or streamer. Others used their software skills to create applications that make Smash events run efficiently. Many of them have become so interested in what the future of esports has to offer, utilizing the skills they've learned, whether inside or outside of school, to make a career of themselves (using the literal definition of career this time). Even if their passions outside of Smash have nothing to do with a career in esports, the mindset developed from the journey of one's Smash career will always be evident.

Through Smash I was able to both meet and play against the famous YouTube singer and third place winner on *The Voice*, Christina "Zurplox" Grimmie who played Ness in Smash 4. I had always listened to her YouTube covers and originals, even blasting some of her music in my earphones while competing in tournaments, ever since I discovered her cover of *Just a Dream* back in 2010. She was as personable in real life as she was in her videos and online. I had the fortunate opportunity to offer her some advice in Smash after the few friendlies we played; in return for all the amazing music she had given the world. I promised that when she would come to perform on tour in San Diego, I would book a VIP ticket and get to know her more in her meet-and-greet. Unfortunately, I was never able to keep that promise, as she had passed away due to an unfortunate shooting in Orlando in a meet-and-greet immediately after her own concert in June 2016, at a way-too-young age of 22. Unfortunately, this isn't the only known death in the community either. No matter what happens, whoever the victim may be, the Smash community have always come together to give each other all the support the victims need. Rest in peace, Zurplox.

Through this video game, I have had the most enriching experiences I've had in my life to date, even without any consoles around. I shared my Smash adventures with travelers I've encountered, whether they play Smash or not. I ate at an oyster bar in New Orleans and shared stories with the man sitting next to me, where we talked about an array of topics from esports and ZeRo's win streak (literally the day before the streak was broken) to his life as a marathon runner. I shared a hostel with the kindest travelers in Orlando, where many were visiting for the theme parks to enjoy a well-deserved summer. I taught a young couple about the future of esports after taking their photo in Times Square, and I walked along the National Mall in Washington D.C. with a couple who noticed the Twitch logo on my shirt. I shared a ride with friends as we suffered through lectures from the Uber driver in Dallas who ridiculed my travel stories for video games because he had a son my age[1]. I shared my dreams and passions in Smash with every single customer at a ramen shop in Boston, performing the best I had ever performed the next day. I've been asked by homeless individuals in Chicago for spare change, which led to an intimate lunch over my first experience with deep-dish pizza. I ventured a 42-hour train ride from there in Chicago back to Los Angeles, sharing laughs with a bartender from New Mexico, an aspiring musician going back home, an IT technician from San Francisco, and many more.

Throughout my writing sessions for this book at Starbucks and other cafes, I shared what I was working on with my baristas and others

---

1   The driver literally laughed "Ha! ... ha! ... HA!" in front of me and three of my friends in the same car. I happened to be sitting in the passenger seat. My friends all felt so sorry for me, but oddly enough I didn't seem to mind. After all, in the end the driver really just had good intentions, though the execution probably could have been... better.

who sat next to me, one time even meeting a fellow Smash player but in Melee instead. I also had the pleasure of informing them that I was in fact not working on a high school project but instead working on this personal project I've been wanting to complete for the longest time while juggling both my engineering career and my Smash career. I'd like to thank them all, if they ever cross fates with this book, for their interest proved that this book would be interesting enough of a story to tell and share the world.

Smash is an art form and we just want to make cool things with our canvas. We're trying to be creative in every match, coming up with new techniques and combos and just enjoying ourselves while trying to be the cool kid for the day. We just want to be great artists and share our art with the world. It's the small, intimate interactions we bond over when we share our art with the people we meet, the impact we leave on each other's lives, that makes Smash awe-inspiring.

I hope that this book inspires the world that amazing things can happen even though "it's just a video game." I hope people can see how important the future of Smash and esports is becoming to the society and how it affects the people around them. I hope that people realize that a video game can literally mean an entire person's livelihood. I hope if anything this helps people to get out there, find their passion, meet new people, work hard, play hard, and just enjoy life as they try to become the best person they can be. From the triumphs to the failures, from the friendships to the travels, from introductions to the parting of paths, Smash is life, and life is beautiful. Let's give it our all. Let's make the sickest plays. Let's make life worth living.

What Now?

Thanks so much for reading! I had never expected this book to become what it is today, let alone having it actually become a real, physical book (or an ebook in your e-reader) in your hands. I had started writing this book near the end of 2015, after my trip to *MLG World Finals*, trying to make this book 99% about how Smash benefits our lives. Over the past three years of adding and revising, Smash 4 turned out to be a roller coaster for everyone involved. I didn't expect to travel so often. I didn't expect Civil War. I didn't expect to actually reach any of my accomplishments. It became more 50% teachings, 50% memoir, and from all the experiences I've been through in the past few years, the latter formed into words way too naturally despite this being my first book. That said, I didn't expect to publish this book right at the end of Smash 4's lifespan either. *Super Smash Bros. Ultimate* caught us all off guard with its announcement trailer back in March 2018; we didn't expect Smash 4 to live so short, especially compared to how large the gaps between other Smash games are (aside from 64 to Melee, which was only two years).

It's been a crazy journey, and I'm so glad you were able to join me on this ride, whether you've competed in Smash tournaments or if you just finished reading this book.

The most insane thing about all of this is that this is only Smash 4. *Super Smash Bros. Ultimate* has just been released, and it's going to be bigger than ever. Four years of Smash 4 was only the beginning. Who knows what'll happen? Maybe I'll even write a second book.

If you want to keep up to date with my Smash adventures going into Ultimate, check out my social media! I'll be writing posts about my travels on my blog (www.kevinkaywho.com), chatting with the Smash community on Twitter (@kevinkaywho), and sharing photos of the places I go on Instagram (@kevinkaywho). Feel free to contact me privately as well through my email (hello@kevinkaywho.com). Regardless of where to find me, I'm always up for a conversation about this amazing game, and I'd love to help you become a part of it all if you're at the ever least interested, whether you want to compete, watch, or just follow the news. Hope to see you around!

Acknowledgments

My thanks to:

Shaun Snieder for sticking with this absurd endeavor for the past three years, from editing the first month of writing to suddenly being put on the spot the final month before publishing (and keeping it a secret this entire time!). It was great for bouncing off ideas and catching Smash jargon that no professional editor could catch.

My Smash crew, Hold it Down!, from the Pillar of Charge to taking me in with welcome arms every time I return to Hawaii for a visit. Hanging out with you guys, whether in person or 2,000 miles away online, is always a blast.

Bobby Kuraya for leading the Hawaii Smash community for the past decade. From taking FTL and I under your wing way back then to becoming partnered with Twitch, it's been a ride, hasn't?

The rest of the Hawaii Smash community. I've visited literally dozens of other regional Smash communities, and there really isn't anything like the aloha here.

The San Diego Smash community. I moved from Hawaii to San Diego without knowing a single person, and without you guys I wouldn't have a social life. From the carpools to the CHON concerts, it's been a fantastic three years of living here. Sorry for grabbing and banana-camping you guys every single tournament.

The rest of the Southern California, or SoCal, Smash community. Whenever I'm able to carpool to MSM (Mega Smash Mondays) or FPF (Falcon Punch Fridays), you guys make the 2+ hour long round-trip rides to Orange County worth it.

The DK Discord. Best online community I've been in, hands down. Not only have I learned so much, but it's always a blast to just hang out with so many like-minded lab monsters. I didn't even ask to be a mod, and the next thing I knew everyone started adding the "iDK" prefix to their display names.

Everyone I've encountered along my travels, especially those who I still talk to on Twitter. You guys are the reason why I can play friendlies for literally over 15 hours throughout a major, and why traveling out-of-region is always a blast whether I travel with a group or by myself.

And of course I couldn't leave this one out—you! If you're a part of the Smash community, thanks to your support we can make this community bigger than ever. If you're not, I *especially* thank you for taking interest in this rather niche hobby and/or career, and I hope you learned a lot from this book!

About the Competitor

In Smash 4, Kevin, or "iDK," is a *Donkey Kong Country* specialist as he competes with both Donkey Kong and Diddy Kong; he intends on adding King K. Rool to his roster in Ultimate. His Donkey Kong is most known for the use of "bidou" controls, which allows movement options like never seen before. His greatest wins include against over five ranked players in San Diego, four ranked players in Southern California, a top-ten player from Northern California, two ranked players in Utah, a top-three player from New Hampshire, and a top-three player from New England (all given their ranks during the season iDK played them). He peaked at 9th on the San Diego Power Ranking and is arguably considered a top-ten Donkey Kong player in the nation.

iDK has traveled to a significant number of national-level tournaments, including *GENESIS, EVO, CEO, Super Smash Con, Shine*, almost every 2GGaming event including *Civil War* and *Hyrule Saga, Frostbite*, multiple *DreamHack* events, and many more. Out of these tournaments, his highest placings include 97th out of 1,272 at *Super*

Smash Con 2016, 65th out of 659 entrants at *Shine 2017*, and 129th out of 1,358 at *EVO 2018*.

Outside of competition, iDK is a moderator for the official Smash 4 and Ultimate Donkey Kong *Discord* servers where he's actively involved in analyzing and theorizing the next tournament match with Donkey Kong. He also moderates several *Twitch* streams including Hawaii Smash 4's channel: @theodofaction.

About the Author

Kevin Hu is a software engineer who spends his free time aspiring to become a notable *Super Smash Bros.* competitor, specifically in *Super Smash Bros. for Wii U* (or *Smash 4*) and *Super Smash Bros. Ultimate.* Born and raised in Oahu, Hawaii, he moved in 2015 to San Diego, California, after graduating from the University of Hawaii at Manoa with a B.S. in Computer Engineering and a B.A. in Studio Art with a focus on graphic design. Now that he lives in the continental states, whenever an opportunity arises, Kevin will always attend tournaments to meet new people and socialize, to become a stronger player, and to explore the world, whether it be the weekly local tournament or the next big national tournament across the country.

When Kevin isn't programming or gaming, he's either creating something in the hobbyist art world from graphic design to drawings to writing the next book, reading books and learning about the world, or coming up with the next dad joke to share on social media to live up to the pun in his gamer tag. Occasionally he'll go for something adventurous, from skydiving to running a marathon to catching a train across the country.